1427

P9-EDW-617

Disaster Recovery: Contingency Planning and Program Evaluation

31.50

ALSO FROM QED®

MANAGEMENT
Planning Techniques for Systems Management
Strategic Planning for Information Systems
Applying Business Planning Techniques to Information Systems
Managing for Productivity in Data Processing
Effective Methods of EDP Quality Assurance
Managing Systems Maintenance
A Guide to EDP Performance Management
The Handbook for Data Center Management
The Data Center Disaster Consultant
Handbook for Data Processing Educators
Time Is of the Essence: The DP Professional's Guide to Getting the Right Things Done
The DP Executive's Guide to Microcomputer Management and Control

TECHNICAL
Computer Control and Audit
Humanizing Office Automation: The Impact of Ergonomics on Productivity
Handbook of Screen Format Design
Architecture and Implementation of Large Scale IBM Computer Systems
1001 Questions and Answers to Help You Prepare for the CDP® Exam
Handbook of COBOL Techniques
High Level COBOL Programming
Humanized Input: Techniques for Reliable Keyed Input
CICS/VS Command Level Reference Guide for COBOL Programmers
EDP System Development Guidelines
Data Analysis: The Key to Data Base Design
The Complete Guide to Software Testing

DATA BASE
Data Base Management Systems for the Eighties
Creating and Planning the Corporate Data Base System Project
Data Base Techniques: Software Selection and Systems Development
IMS Design and Implementation Techniques
CODASYL Data Base Management Systems: Design Fundamentals
The Data Base Monograph Series
Data Base Systems: A Practical Reference
Information Resource/Data Dictionary Systems
Managing Database: Four Critical Factors

TELECOMM/DATA COMM
Transnational Data Regulation: The Realities
Distributed Processing: Current Practice and Future Developments

THE QED® PERSONAL COMPUTING SERIES
The IBM Personal Computer: What You Should Know
Learning to Use the IBM Personal Computer
How to Buy Software for Personal Computers
Peachtree Software for Personal Computers: Introduction & Description
The Complete Guide to Installing Personal Computers

THE CHANTICO TECHNICAL MANAGEMENT SERIES
Strategic and Operational Planning for Information Systems
Security Evaluation for Small Computer Centers
Disaster Recovery: Contingency Planning and Program Evaluation
Reviewing the Operation of Small Computer Systems
Management Evaluation of Software Packages

THE QED® EASY LEARNING SERIES
PC PLUS: Learn The IBM PC . . . Plus Computing Fundamentals
DOS Made Easy . . . Learn to Use IBM PC DOS
TYPING Made Easy . . . Learn to Touch Type Quickly and Easily
MultiMate Made Easy
Lotus 1-2-3 Made Easy

FOR INFORMATION, CONTACT:
QED® Information Sciences, Inc. • QED Plaza • P.O. Box 181 • Wellesley, Massachusetts 02181

Disaster Recovery: Contingency Planning and Program Evaluation

THE CHANTICO TECHNICAL MANAGEMENT SERIES

QED® Information Sciences, Inc.
Wellesley, Massachusetts

©1985 by QED Information Sciences, Inc.
QED Plaza o P.O. Box 181
Wellesley, MA 02181

Originally published by The Chantico Publishing Company
Port Jefferson, New York

Library of Congress Number 85-60177

International Standard Book Number 0-89435-152-4

Printed in the United States of America

1

CONTENTS

MANAGEMENT CONSIDERATIONS
IN EDP DISASTER RECOVERY PLANNING

i

FIGURES

DISASTER RECOVERY PROGRAM EVALUATOR

Section   **Page**

Part II – Conducting the Review Program

Part III - Evaluating the Disaster Recovery Program

FIGURES

1

MANAGEMENT CONSIDERATIONS IN EDP

DISASTER RECOVERY PLANNING

MANAGEMENT CONSIDERATIONS
IN EDP DISASTER RECOVERY PLANNING

SECTION 1

INTRODUCTION

SECTION OVERVIEW

This section is a management summary of the objectives of, and the need for, an EDP Disaster Recovery Plan. Such a plan is an organized effort to minimize the impact of a possible disaster that may interrupt the data processing capabilities of an organization.

The management of every organization must look at what the consequences of loss of their EDP resources could be, and consider their exposure. Three areas of exposure that management should review are: financial loss, legal responsibility, and business service interruption.

This manual is concerned with management considerations in the preparation of a Disaster Recovery Plan, in the development of such a plan, and in the installation and testing of it. The manual presents a program and a methodology and describes the roles that various parts of the organization must accept in disaster recovery readiness. Checklists and worksheets are provided to assist management in understanding and reviewing their areas of concern.

1

1.1 OBJECTIVES OF AN EDP DISASTER RECOVERY PLAN

The objectives of an EDP Disaster Recovery Plan are to make sufficient agreed upon preparations, and to design and implement a sufficient set of agreed upon procedures, for responding to a disaster of any size in Information Services. The purpose of these agreed upon procedures is to minimize the effect of a disaster upon the operations of the organization. The emphasis should be on safeguarding the vital assets of the organization and ensuring the continued availability of critical EDP services.

The preparations and procedures should be well understood by the staff. The plan should specify the responsibilities to be handled both before and after a disaster, and document them in a manual which is distributed to, and used by, all supervisory personnel. It should define the basic approach, state the assumptions and priorities, and point up areas of particular concern.

In the event of a disaster in any part of the organization served by the EDP facilities, or dependent on Information Services operations, the plan must be workable for activation on short notice. It must encompass all phases of the migration to and operations at the backup sites, should that prove necessary. Sections of the plan must be usable for responses to minor emergencies. After initial acceptance of the plan by management, it must be possible to schedule complete or partial "disaster drills" to activate and test the backup capability.

A "disaster" is any security event which can cause a significant disruption in the Information Services capabilities for long enough to affect the operations of the organization. It means any situation which leaves the EDP facility in a non-productive state. A Disaster Recovery Plan, then, may also be called a Contingency Plan, or an Emergency Management Plan.

Procedures to recover from a disaster are written for the most probable serious occurrence of a security event. Events of lesser magnitude can be handled at the appropriate level, as a subset of the recovery procedures.

1.2 NEED FOR AN EDP DISASTER RECOVERY PLAN

Security measures are employed to prevent or detect accidental or intentional disclosure, modification, or destruction of data, or the loss of the means of processing data. Disaster Recovery Plans are designed to reduce the consequences of the loss of any EDP resources or capability to an acceptable level. They are not merely planned responses to major catastrophes. They are designed to reduce the damaging consequences of unexpected and undesirable events of any magnitude. The greatest probability is that damaging occurrences will be less than catastrophic, and may be confined to smaller areas of the operation. The size and scope of a disaster and its effect on data processing operations are often not directly related, however. For example, a relatively small fire in the computer communications area could be quite catastrophic to the operations, while the loss of some terminals in a completely destroyed building could be recovered rapidly. Data processing operations are so interconnected that there is a need for a Disaster Recovery Plan that covers the whole operation and any individual parts of it.

2

Every organization must look at what the consequences of loss of their EDP resources could be and consider their exposure. It is simply good business practice. There are three areas of exposure that must be reviewed:

- Financial Loss

- Legal Responsibility

- Business Service Interruption

A.   Financial Loss

Because of the efficiency, accuracy, speed, and control of data processing methods, organizations are becoming more and more dependent on their Information Services in normal business operations. The regular, daily operations of large numbers of companies are now completely dependent upon the information flowing from the EDP area. Manufacturing systems, sales and reservations systems, inventory systems, and financial systems, among many others, can no longer revert to manual operations on short notice. An organization's life blood, information, can rapidly dry up if the EDP systems break down. This can cause great financial loss to a company and could even destroy it if proper disaster planning has not been done.

EDP disaster recovery planning takes steps in advance to ensure the continuity of business information if the EDP capability is lost. It has been estimated that most businesses could survive without EDP for one shift, and probably even one day. By the time three days or a week had passed, however, many businesses would be getting into serious cash flow problems. Within a month without EDP, most businesses would have serious problems of survival. Few modern companies could remain in business today after six months of EDP loss. Large numbers of organizations are highly dependent on their on-line EDP operations to maintain their cash flow.

B.   Legal Responsibility

Management has a legal responsibility to protect its employees, its corporate resources, and its vital documents. One interpretation of the Foreign Corrupt Practices Act of 1977 has been that officers of a company are personally responsible if there have not been adequate preparations to meet these legal requirements.

It is also clear that officers of a company who have not taken the necessary precautions to minimize the effects of a possible disaster are exposing themselves to legal suit in the event of a disaster striking which causes losses that could have been reduced.

C.   Business Service Interruption

The problems of business service interruption do not only include the financial loss discussed above. They also can be deleterious to future relationships with clients. They can affect the public image of the organization for a considerable time. If an organization's business service is abruptly interrupted, for reasons not readily perceived by customers, the long-term effect could be devastating and far more costly than modest preparations for disaster recovery.

3

If the service is based on a contract with the government, it could well be a contractual requirement that reasonable precautions to maintain the continuity of the service have been planned and taken.

It is simply good business practice to make contingency preparations to reduce the consequences of any security event. Management must be confident that their data processing capability can be depended upon.

MANAGEMENT CONSIDERATIONS
IN EDP DISASTER RECOVERY PLANNING

SECTION 2

MANAGEMENT CONSIDERATIONS

SECTION OVERVIEW

This section discusses the basic management considerations relative to an EDP Disaster Recovery Plan, and the method of approach to develop one. It describes the areas of disaster risk and the levels of security and disaster recovery measures indicated. It suggests the tailoring of a plan to the particular organization.

A key principle of disaster recovery is to limit the chances and effects of a disaster beforehand. This is done by adopting ongoing EDP security practices. Some basic checklists are included to help management ascertain whether they should best first strengthen their security practices, then adopt a recovery plan.

2.1 COMPONENTS OF AN EDP DISASTER RECOVERY PLAN

An EDP Disaster Recovery Plan should include:

- **The EDP Disaster Recovery Plan Report** outlining:

  - Assumptions and Considerations

  - Recovery Requirements

  - Description of all resources reviewed, highlighting the critical resources

  - Strategies Considered and Recommended Strategy

  - Detailed Recovery Procedures

  - Emergency Plan and Backup Plan

  - Staffing and Responsibilities

  - Maintenance and Testing Procedures

- **Recommendations for Actions** to be taken by management to put the plan in place and test it regularly.

- **EDP Disaster Recovery Procedures** giving detailed assignments and locations for actions to be taken at the time of an emergency until the backup operation is running.

- **Recovery and Restoration Procedures** to return to the original site or another one selected by management.

- **Documentation and Related Information** as an Appendix which may not be included with most copies of the plan.

2.2 PRELIMINARY MANAGEMENT CONCERNS

The purpose of EDP disaster recovery planning is to prepare in advance to ensure the continuity of business information if the EDP capability is lost. Thus, disaster recovery planning, particularly as it is being planned and started, is a management rather than a technical issue. It deals with the realities of people, organizational relationships, and special interests. Disaster recovery actions are highly prioritized, and many normal operations are neglected. Management must take the lead and continually assess the technical considerations involved as to their utility.

Some of the considerations for management are listed below.

A. Evaluating the Need Realistically

Management must realize that EDP professionals agree there are no completely secure computers. Many computer operations have fine methods for security in place, and management can be assured that the best possible actions have been taken; but there are always people, electronics, and natural disasters that can suddenly disrupt the operations. Management must realistically look at:

- Legal Obligation Requirements

- Cash Flow Maintenance

- Customer Services

- Competitive Advantages

- Production and Distribution Decisions

- Logistics and Operations Control

- Purchasing Functions and Vendor Relationships

- Ongoing Project Control

- Branch or Agency Communications

- Personnel and Union Relations

- Shareholder and Public Relations

Management must assess the importance of EDP operations to these facets of their business, then decide the type of effort that should be put into backup of the EDP function.

B. Providing Organizational Commitment

Management must provide organizational commitment to the development and maintenance of a disaster recovery plan. This must include:

- Funding the Planning and Maintenance

- Assignment of Internal Staff

- Obtaining the Interest of Senior Management

- Getting Cooperation from the User Departments

- Involving All Related Departments, such as Security, Buildings, Purchasing, etc.

- Setting Planning Priorities

- Reviewing the Planning during Development

- Considering the Use of Consulting Support

- Ensuring Continuing Commitment once the Plan is in Place

- Periodic Testing of the Plan

- Integration of the Plan in the Normal Business Process

C.   Interfacing with Existing Policies and Programs

Management must consider how the EDP Disaster Recovery Plan will interface with existing organizational policies and procedures. There may already be a disaster planning guide for the overall business. In this case, the EDP guide should fit into it. Most organizations have plans in place for at least some of the following:

- Fire Protection Equipment Installation and Maintenance

- Emergency Fire Alarm Procedures

- Fire Monitor or Instructor Training

- Guard Duties, Training, and Procedures

- Relationships with External Emergency Alarm Services

- Relationships with Local Fire and Police Departments

- Bomb Threat Procedures

- Strike or Mob Threat Procedures

- Storm Emergency Information and Restoration Plans

- Emergency Control Centers

These are all supportive of EDP recovery, and management must see that the EDP plans fit with them.

D.   Setting Up the Study and Planning Group

Management must consider how to set up the study and planning group so that the many facets of an EDP disaster plan may be fully assembled. A great deal of technical work must be done by people such as the Systems Programming Group. Without their work, there will be no operable plan. However, they are not normally in a position to know the priorities required. The users will all feel they must have high priority and will be dismayed when they are low on the list. Because of these and other pressures, a strong study team must be set up that can understand both the technical

8

and business aspects. Good people must be chosen to make a "plan for the plan" and indicate the problem areas that will need management attention.

Management must then cooperate with planning, and provide the funding and the open doors to accomplish the task. One of the best steps to take early is to appoint a competent, experienced person as EDP Security Coordinator (or Administrator, or Director). This person can then coordinate the plan development, testing, and ongoing maintenance.

E.   **Involving Internal Audit**

Internal Audit should be involved as an integral part of the EDP disaster recovery planning process at the points where it is deemed most fruitful for them to contribute. Some areas can be:

- **Checking the Ongoing EDP Security Practices**
  They would not necessarily use only the attached checklists but may go deeper into the analysis of the practices.

- **Accepting a Staff Assignment on the Team**
  They have a strong part to play in establishing the necessary controls to be installed in the routine backup of files and during a disaster recovery operation. It can be very difficult to maintain audit trails at such times.

- **Reviewing the Vital Record Requirements**
  This is a fundamental area requiring stringent fiscal control.

- **Reviewing the Risk Analysis Calculations**
  These calculations may be basic to the justification of the project. If they are not needed, the overriding operational necessity should be reviewed.

- **Planning the Management of Resources**

- **Consideration of Salvage Handling and Value**
  The Insurance Group will want their evaluation of the salvage.

- **Refereeing the Tests of the Recovery Procedures**
  Good technical procedures and smooth computer operations do not necessarily indicate a good recovery in a controlled manner.

- **Ongoing Monitoring and Periodic Testing**
  They should be in charge of the timing, areas tested, and evaluation of results.

2.3   PRIORITY CONCERNS OF MANAGEMENT

The principal area of concern in disaster recovery operations must be the safety and well-being of the personnel involved. The principal business concern is the maintenance of accounting records and customer services. The business interruption loss must be kept as low as possible, and the required cash flow maintained. Legal and reporting requirements must, of course, be maintained also.

An additional fundamental concern is the protection of facilities, equipment, programs, and supplies. **Figure 2-1, Disaster Recovery Priority Concerns of Management,** expands on these concerns. Management can use it to check the fundamental, minimum requirements.

2.4   LEVELS OF SECURITY AND DISASTER RECOVERY MEASURES

A Disaster Recovery Plan is developed to minimize the costs resulting from losses of, or damages to, the resources or the capabilities of an EDP facility and related services. It is dependent for success on the recognition of the potential consequences of undesirable happenings. There are many resources related to Information Services operations. Some particular subset of these is required to support each function that is provided to others in the organization. These resources include: people, programs, data, EDP hardware, communications equipment and systems, electric power, the physical facility and access to it, and even items such as paper forms.

All resources are not equally important, nor are they equally susceptible to harm. The selection of safeguards and the elements of a contingency plan should, therefore, be done with an informed awareness of which system functions are supported by each resource element, and of the susceptibility of each element to harm. The cost-effective protection of an EDP operation is thus dependent on:

- The importance to the organization of each of the component parts of the EDP functions.

- The general probability of something undesirable happening to each of the components.

- The likely results and ramifications of various types of disasters that could occur.

- Preparations that can be made to minimize the chances of disasters, and the costs if they do occur.

Any part of a Disaster Recovery Plan is overhead cost until it becomes necessary to activate it. It is, therefore, necessary to consider the importance of the resources and services and to justify each security and disaster recovery measure by estimating the losses that could occur through lack of these precautions. The combination of initial expenditures and insurance coverage must be balanced against the necessity of the service and the probability of the need of the recovery procedures. There are some actions that are mandatory, however. They must be taken, whatever the cost.

Figure 2-1
(Page 1)

DISASTER RECOVERY PRIORITY CONCERNS OF MANAGEMENT

No.	Item	Yes	No	N/A
	Staff Protection and Actions			
1.	Have all staff been trained in fire alarm, bomb threat, and other emergency procedures?			
2.	Do all staff understand that when the alarm sounds they:			
	● Immediately vacate the building?			
	● Do not return to pick up items from desks?			
	● Report to supervisors at designated points?			
3.	Do all staff know who to call in times of emergency or where the emergency telephone list is located?			
4.	Do the disaster recovery planning teams understand that the protection and safety of people in the area is paramount?			
5.	Have good management notification procedures been developed for any emergency of any size?			
	Maintenance of Customer Services and Cash Flow			
6.	Has management strictly prioritized the most necessary services to be maintained in an emergency?			
7.	Are all user groups involved in customer services and cash handling working with the plan teams?			
8.	For on-line customer services, can alternate operations be brought up within 24 hours?			
9.	Are most cash deposits sent directly to banks and not vulnerable to a disaster in the computer area?			
10.	Does the organization have plans for controlled public press releases in times of disaster?			

Figure 2-1
(Page 2)

DISASTER RECOVERY PRIORITY CONCERNS OF MANAGEMENT

No.	Item	Yes	No	N/A
	Maintenance of Vital Documents			
11.	Have the vital documents and records of the organization been thoroughly analyzed and control procedures set up?			
12.	Does the organization use a remote, safe document storage vault?			
13.	Is there extensive use of Computer Output Microfilm/Microfiche or the microfilming of documents, and are copies stored in a safe vault?			
14.	Are application and operations documentation of programs handling vital information backed up in safe storage?			
15.	Is the Legal Department satisfied with the EDP handling of vital documents?			
	Protection of Facilities, Equipment, Programs, and Supplies			
16.	Are the organization's Fire, Safety, and Engineering people working closely with Information Services?			
17.	Have the fire and safety systems in the EDP facility area been reviewed by an independent person?			
18.	Have discussions been held with all equipment vendors as to their response to an emergency situation?			
19.	Has there been a recent review of the documentation level of programs and the existence of updated backup copies of the programs and the documentation?			
20.	Is there a complete listing of all supplies and copies of all forms available in a second site, and are emergency backups of critical forms held in a second site?			

There are three levels of security and disaster recovery measures that should be considered in balancing cost to need. These are:

- Mandatory Measures

- Necessary Measures

- Desirable Measures

There is no absolute scale, and these measures will vary as conditions change. Management must review what is mandatory and necessary for their organization, support those efforts first, and then consider the justification analysis of desirable measures. These measures are outlined below.

A.   Mandatory Measures

Mandatory security and disaster recovery measures are those related to fire control, alarm systems, evacuation procedures, and other emergency precautions necessary to protect the lives and well-being of people in the area involved. Mandatory measures also include those needed to protect the books of account of the organization, and to hold its officers free from legal negligence. The protection must include the assets of the organization as much as possible. The cost of these mandatory measures must be included in the cost of doing business. The items must also be reviewed periodically as to routine operation and adequacy. They should be reviewed with organization counsel.

B.   Necessary Measures

Necessary security and disaster recovery measures include all reasonable precautions taken to prevent serious disruption of the operation of the organization. This will include selected areas of:

- Manufacturing and Distribution

- Engineering and Planning

- Sales and Marketing

- Employee Relations, and so on.

The necessity of the measures must be determined by senior management, who should also review their understanding of the need periodically. Since the necessary measures will be included in the base operating cost of the organization, each selected measure must be reviewed as to both degree and speed of emergency backup required.

C.   Desirable Measures

Desirable security and disaster recovery measures include reasonable precautions taken to prevent real inconvenience or disruption to any area of the organization, and to keep the business under smooth control. The cost of some precautions related to personnel is small, but planned action is important to maintain operational efficiency and morale. The cost of other measures, such as arrangements for alternate sites for systems and programming personnel and their terminals, may be large. Estimates and plans must be made, however, to allow reasonable and cost-effective management decisions once the extent of a disaster is understood.

The mandatory measures should be implemented as soon as possible. The necessary measures should be implemented in order of priority with a definite plan approved by senior management. The desirable measures should be implemented as circumstances allow. Cost is balanced against perceived need and desirability.

2.5 PLAN TAILORED TO THE ORGANIZATION

An EDP Disaster Recovery Plan must be specific to the organization and tailored to its needs. An off-the-shelf plan is of no use whatsoever at the time of a security event when individuals need to know exactly what their role is and the steps they must take. The presence of a "paper plan" does not in itself provide a disaster recovery capability. All people in the organization who may be involved in a recovery activity should also be involved in the plan preparation, training, and testing.

A. Initial Short-Term, High-Impact Plan

The disaster recovery planning process can require many months and enormous activity if the full process is carried out exhaustively, including:

- Review of All Data Sets and Data Files

- Discussion with All Users

- Complete Assembly of All Documentation

- Full Risk Identification and Risk Analysis Study

- Detailed Review of Ongoing EDP Security Practices

Such an approach could be self-defeating as it could be very costly and time-consuming, and management would lose interest in supporting it. It would also put off the installation of mandatory and necessary security measures that are most critical to the organization.

The better approach for the initial effort is for a small team to gather under the direction of a senior EDP manager and make a short-term, high impact plan to get something in place that will handle the most pressing needs and have high visibility. The steps they should take are:

1. Assemble all readily available operations and systems documentation.

2. Assemble the reports of any audits or security studies of the EDP functions.

3. Create lists of the operating application systems in the first estimation of the order of priority, divided by major organization functions.

4. Consult with senior management in the financial, administrative, and operational areas to get their opinions as to the mandatory and necessary applications in an agreed order of priority.

5. Work with Systems Programming and Operations to see that all such systems are backed up at least daily and stored in a secure site.

6. Determine the minimum configuration on which these mandatory and necessary systems can run (it may be more than one computer) and arrange for tests.

7. Determine if these critical systems can be backed up and run off-site in an emergency in the time required.

8. Keep management informed of the results and, when the tests are completed, ask for a full study to be funded to cover all security factors and all applications.

It is important to take less than six months to produce a viable backup capability for the critical systems and do preliminary tests on it. This should have the visibility and impact needed to get support for a more comprehensive study and capability.

B. Full Disaster Recovery Project Plan

If it is desired to have a full EDP Disaster Recovery project, culminating in a comprehensive plan that includes all facets of the EDP operations, the organization and the "plan-for-the-plan" must be carefully assembled. The disaster recovery study project must be handled as any other systems development project and be broken into phases which are planned for individually. The elements of such a project are given in **Figure 2-2, EDP Disaster Recovery Project Plan.** This project plan has been designed to divide the effort into six familiar phases for ready reporting to management and for keeping the study under control. These phases are:

    I.   Definition Phase

    II.   Functional Requirements Phase

    III.   Design and Development Phase

    IV.   Implementation Phase

    V.   Testing and Monitoring Phase

    VI.   Maintenance Phase

Figure 2-2
(Page 1)

EDP DISASTER RECOVERY PROJECT PLAN

I. **Definition Phase**

    1. Decide on disaster recovery objectives.

    2. Appoint EDP Security Coordinator and Planning Team.

    3. Develop initial set of assumptions and definitions.

    4. Decide on types of disaster to consider.

    5. Tentatively select a Key Disaster Scenario.

II. **Functional Requirements Phase**

    1. Assemble all organizational procedures and standards relative to emergencies.

    2. Assemble all documentation relative to the inventory of resources, including hardware, communications, software, forms, facility descriptions, etc.

    3. Make an evaluation of what systems are mandatory, necessary, or desirable.

    4. Analyze the applications and facilities against the recovery objectives.

    5. Decide on long-term strategy or short-term, high-impact plan.

    6. Assess the operational requirements of the critical resources and applications.

    7. Agree on the assumptions and definitions.

    8. Tentatively determine what is to be covered in the plan.

    9. Set priorities and acceptable timeframes for recovery.

Figure 2-2
(Page 2)

EDP DISASTER RECOVERY PROJECT PLAN

III. **Design and Development Phase**

1. Decide on the requirements for the critical resources and applications.

2. Evaluate alternative recovery strategies.

3. Select one or more specific recovery strategies.

4. Perform a cost/benefit analysis for the management report.

5. Perform a full risk analysis, if appropriate.

6. Decide on the organization for Disaster Recovery Teams.

7. Plan the management of resources during a disaster event.

8. Identify potential vendors and price their services.

9. Select the final design and prepare detailed recovery procedures.

10. Produce the Plan report with recommendations.

IV. **Implementation Phase**

1. Acquire any hardware, software, communications lines, etc. that are needed.

2. Negotiate and sign contracts with vendors.

3. Get agreement on final, detailed procedures.

4. Train personnel.

5. Prepare sites.

6. Develop test and monitoring plans.

7. Develop maintenance plan.

Figure 2-2
(Page 3)

EDP DISASTER RECOVERY PROJECT PLAN

V. **Testing and Monitoring Phase**

1. Set up test plan with Internal Audit.

2. Schedule tests for small sections of the plan at a time.

3. Make arrangements to use facilities external to your organization.

4. Attempt to run backup systems.

5. Analyze the backup output compared to the normal operations.

6. Correct errors in the plan.

7. Repeat a variety of tests periodically.

VI. **Maintenance Phase**

1. Develop a system to update names, responsibilities, and telephone numbers.

2. See that system for backup libraries is working smoothly.

3. Standardize documentation and procedures.

C.   Long-Term Strategy

The long-term EDP strategy for disaster recovery should seek to create an understanding of the need for the plans and procedures, just as people understand the need for fire alarm procedures. The long-term strategy should be directed towards creating a full, effective disaster recovery capability by:

- Assigning a full-time person or persons.

- Assigning task groups that report regularly to management.

- Obtaining budget funding for a practical capability.

- Involving all organizational groups, such as security, guards, buildings, insurance, engineers, etc.

- Developing a full disaster recovery capability covering all areas of Information Services.

- Having regular training of all staff in the plan actions.

- Testing the plan realistically and regularly in cooperation with the Internal Audit Group.

2.6   ONGOING EDP SECURITY PRACTICES

A.   Controls, Standards, and Procedures

It is axiomatic that the best plan for disaster recovery is to prevent the occurrence of disasters in the first place. The cost of prevention is far less than the cost of cure. It is generally agreed by experts in the field, however, that there are no completely secure computers. An astute manager will, therefore, balance the costs of installing as many security precautions as are reasonable, offset by creating a full disaster recovery plan that can handle nearly all foreseen occurrences.

The first principle of disaster recovery is:

- Review, examine, and strengthen all basic EDP security controls, standards, and procedures.

This activity can be done before, during, or after the installation and imple-mentation of the first high-impact, short-term plan. Clearly, it should be done on a continuing basis. Ongoing EDP security practices are the foundation upon which disaster recovery must be built.

There are a number of manuals on the market that contain security checklists. Many articles have been written about them. Many consultants are pleased to bring their own checklists on site. Three of the finest and most comprehensive manuals that cover this area are FTP publications:

- Auditing Computer Systems

- Internal Controls:

    Volume I - Design, Maintenance, and Assessment
    Volume II - Control Descriptions

- EDP Security - Data/Facilities/Personnel

    Volume I - EDP Security Planning and Implementation
    Volume II - EDP Security Testing and Review

These manuals are available from the FTP Technical Library, 492 Old Town Road, Port Jefferson Station, New York 11776. Telephone: (516) 473-1110.

B. Name Specific Individuals, Locations, and Actions

In tailoring the plan to the organization, a key necessity is to name specific individuals with their responsibilities, locations where tasks will be accomplished, and actions to take in priority sequence. It is possible to name positions rather than people if there is a handy directory available, but it is not as effective. Positions do not have home telephone numbers, but people do. Individuals should be quite familiar with whom they are calling in a "telephone tree," and be able to call them even if they have misplaced their emergency lists. Key people should take their copies of the plans home to have them available nights and weekends. These names and phone numbers should be updated regularly.

Similarly, in time of disaster emergency, management should not be sitting down at tables wondering where to send their staff. This should all have been worked out in advance for at least one scenario with suggestions and office plans easily available for other scenarios. Everyone should be able to operate at such times with minimal direction. They should know in advance where they are going and where to make arrangements for others. They should also all have a good understanding of the minimal actions for which they will be responsible and the best priority order to take such actions.

MANAGEMENT CONSIDERATIONS
IN EDP DISASTER RECOVERY PLANNING

SECTION 3

PERSONNEL PARTICIPATION IN THE PLAN

SECTION OVERVIEW

This section describes the commitment needed from senior management. It also points out that all organizational groups that may be affected or needed in any way must be brought into the planning phase. It outlines some of the assignments and responsibilities of different groups.

The need for appointing an EDP Security Coordinator (or Administrator or Officer) is emphasized. This person should chair the planning teams and have the ongoing responsibility of keeping the plan up-to-date.

It is suggested that recovery operations be handled by "teams" with specific responsibilities. Some examples are listed. The key team is the Initial Response Management Team, which is the first to review the security event, and to make the needed decisions regarding the level of response.

The EDP Security Coordinator works with the leaders of all the teams to develop the described "plan for the plan."

3.1   SENIOR MANAGEMENT COMMITMENT

The reasons for an organization to have an EDP Disaster Recovery Plan are clear, and most of them affect senior management directly. They include:

- Maintenance of Cash Flow

- Protection of Vital Records

- Maintenance of Customer Service

- Freedom from Suit because of Operations Disruption

- Meeting the Requirements of the Foreign Corrupt Practices Act of 1977

- Protection of Employees

Because of the sensitivity of the subject, senior management should probably not be approached for support until EDP management has a good idea of how strong their security is and what may be involved in a disaster recovery program. On the other hand, disaster recovery planning is a management, rather than a technical, issue. It deals with the realities of people, politics, and special interests. It cannot be accomplished properly without senior management support, and senior management must be approached as early as possible after the EDP management feels comfortable with the issues involved.

In most organizations, there are many groups who will have a direct interest in the EDP disaster planning. These can include:

Security	Labor Relations
Medical	Transportation
Finance	Personnel
Legal	Buildings
Audit	Engineering
Public Relations	All the User Departments

There is no way these groups can all be made to work in concert without strong senior management commitment and a formal plan for action which has been approved.

3.2   APPOINTMENT OF EDP SECURITY COORDINATOR

This position goes by a number of titles:

- EDP Security Coordinator

- EDP Security Administrator

- EDP Director of Security

- Data Security Officer (DSO) in the government

The title given will depend on organizational policies and the size of the group to be formed. In small EDP facilities, it may well be an extra job for an existing position. The position is required, however, to give visibility, continuity, and funding for the work to be done, particularly on an ongoing basis. The appointment is best made at the time of the task force studies so that the person can readily become familiar with all aspects of the plan and the reasons for the various decisions.

Some of the duties of an EDP Security Coordinator will include:

1. Taking responsibility for following up on the preplanning required to create the Disaster Recovery Plan.

2. Assembling information on EDP disaster recovery, and keep files on vendors of all sorts.

3. Working closely with Internal Audit to test security measures and disaster recovery plans, and reporting on the results to management.

4. Maintaining the plan on an ongoing basis, keeping the documentation updated, and, particularly, correcting names, addresses, and telephone numbers.

5. Investigating other Information Services security problems that cross departmental lines.

6. Checking periodically with outside groups, such as mutual aid groups and vendors, to reaffirm disaster aid arrangements.

7. Assembling and distributing literature on security and disaster recovery, and attending occasional metings on the subject to keep abreast of the latest advances and thinking.

The EDP Security Coordinator position is primarily a staff job which is management related, but it requires a broad knowledge of EDP technical considerations to understand what Systems Programming, Operations, etc., are doing. It is a good job for a supervisor out of any of the line departments in EDP. Occasionally, it will have high exposure for the individual. It will entail detailed work more closely related to audit than EDP operations.

The "coordination" part of the job will be called for most during the planning phase, when the person must:

1. Chair the planning meetings to see that everyone is headed in the same direction.

2. Follow up with each Team Leader to see that the agreed preplanning tasks are accomplished.

3. Obtain lists of all necessary staff addresses and home telephone numbers, and enter them in the telephone list directories. This may be a sensitive area as many people do not wish to release their home telephone numbers. The key people, at least, must do it.

4. Check on whether schedules for testing sections of the plan have been developed and are being followed.

5. Confirm the Recovery Procedures with each participant, and modify as necessary.

6. See that sufficient copies of the Disaster Recovery Procedures are made up and put into visible binders. (It is preferable to use a bright color.) Distribute these binders and request that Team Leaders take their copies home to be available in the event of an emergency situation.

7. Have critical elements of the Emergency Recovery Procedures put up on the automated documentation system, if one is used, so that it is available at terminals.

3.3 EDP DISASTER RECOVERY PLANNING TEAM

The Planning Team, for creation of the plan to develop the Disaster Recovery Plan (the plan for the plan), will normally be a small group. They will have initial conversations with a number of managers to determine management intent for the plan and the possibilities that first appear to be open to the organization. They will then develop a detailed project plan in the manner which is normal for planning projects in their organization.

A. Detailed Project Plan

The Detailed Project Plan will be developed by the Planning Team to divide the effort into several phases, for ready reporting to management, and for keeping the study under control. These phases could be:

I. Definition Phase (Objectives and Assumptions)

II. Functional Requirements Phase (Fact-Gathering and Decisions)

III. Design and Development Phase (Evaluation of Alternatives)

IV. Implementation Phase (Creating the Plan)

V. Testing and Monitoring Phase (Post-Development Review)

VI. Maintenance Phase (Updating the Plan)

More detail is given on these phases in Figure 2-2, EDP Disaster Recovery Project Plan.

B.   Commitment to the Plan

After the Project Plan has been created, time and cost estimates must be made for its implementation. The Planning Team will have to go to management to determine if there is sufficient commitment to develop an adequate plan. If the commitment is forthcoming, the request can then be made for full-time and part-time assignments for personnel from all parts of the organization. Some may just be required to give interviews, others to make brief studies, and others to do detailed analyses. There will be sufficient effort involved for getting senior management approval at the start. Doors will then be opened as needed.

The EDP Disaster Recovery Planning Team may only need one of their members as a full-time participant, preferably the EDP Security Coordinator. The others can discuss the problems or produce analyses as necessary or assign staff members to do the work.

A good plan will cost considerable money to develop and test. It should not be started as a quick-and-easy project.

C.   Initial Request for Information

One of the first jobs of the EDP Disaster Recovery Planning Team is to gather as much existing documentation as possible and request ideas and comments from the various EDP groups. The team should find that it has very little raw information gathering to do. Most of the information that the team requires should already exist as documentation somewhere in the EDP department. The team should, therefore, rapidly make out lists of Requests for Information tailored to each EDP group and distribute them to the appropriate supervisors. When the time comes to interview these groups and discuss the plan with them, they may not have prepared all the material, but they will have at least started gathering it, and they will know generally what will be needed.

The types of information to be requested will vary greatly between EDP organizations. It will depend on the computers involved, the number of sites, and the work that has already been done on backup storage. The information is simply basic data on what is involved so that the team can grasp the size of the problem, the relationships involved, and a few of the facts. **Figure 3-1, Requests for Information,** presents typical lists of these early requests. These example lists are divided into:

- EDP Operations Documentation

- Application Systems Documentation

- Technical Support Documentation

Figure 3-1
(Page 1)

REQUESTS FOR INFORMATION

EDP OPERATIONS DOCUMENTATION

1. EDP Facility Layouts: All Locations

   - Site Plans, Floor Plans, and Utility Lines

2. Organization Chart

   - List Names plus Addresses and Telephone Numbers of Supervisors

3. Hardware Configurations

4. List of Vendors and Contacts

   - Include Miscellaneous Equipment, Data Entry Equipment, Microfilm, etc.

5. Any Emergency Warning Systems, Emergency Controls, Emergency Communications Systems

6. Any Assigned Responsibilities for Fire, Safety, or Emergency - Company or EDP departments

7. Any Emergency and First Aid Equipment

8. Number of Tape Files

   - Documentation of what is Duplicated and Off-Site

9. Operating Manuals and Written Procedures

   - Including Powering Down, Emergency Shutdown, Safety Rules, etc.

10. Volumes of Supplies Stored and Approximate Weekly Use

Figure 3-1
(Page 2)

REQUESTS FOR INFORMATION

APPLICATION SYSTEMS DOCUMENTATION

1. List of Applications Systems with:

   - Contact Responsibility in EDP Departments and User Departments

   - Processing Requirements and Schedules

     - Number of Terminals Used

   - Program and Data Files

   - Checklist of Documentation

     - List of Programs

     - Control of Documentation

2. List of Development, Maintenance, and Test Work

   - Personnel Assigned

   - Computer Requirements

3. List of Purchased or Leased Systems

   - Vendors and Contacts

4. List of Personnel, Addresses, and Telephone Numbers

Figure 3-1
(Page 3)

REQUESTS FOR INFORMATION

TECHNICAL SUPPORT DOCUMENTATION

1. Systems Software for Computers

   - Checklist of Documentation and Tapes Required

2. Estimation of Choice of Priority Applications on Backup Computer

3. Teleprocessing Plan between Sites

   - Various Alternatives
   - Possible Reconfigurations of Data Entry Network

4. Review Emergency Possibilities of:

   - Moving Some Applications to Timesharing Services
   - Moving Some Applications Batch to Other Computers
   - Other Similar Computers in the Geographic Area

5. Backup Plan for Word Processing Equipment

6. Disaster Coordination with Database Group

7. List of Vendors and Contacts for Systems

8. List of Personnel, Addresses, and Telephone Numbers

Figure 3-1
(Page 4)

REQUESTS FOR INFORMATION

DATABASE ADMINISTRATION DOCUMENTATION

1. General Documentation of Databases

    - Applications on Current and Planned

    - Size and Projected Size

    - Separation of Test and Production Databases

2. Planned Departmental Use of Database

3. List of Equipment and Software Vendor Contacts

4. List of Personnel, Addresses, and Telephone Numbers

Figure 3-1
(Page 5)

REQUESTS FOR INFORMATION

OFFICE SERVICES DOCUMENTATION

1. Company Policy Statements and Positions

   - Emergencies

   - Security

   - Civil Preparedness

2. Company Emergency Communications Plans

3. Plans for Protection of Vital Records and Documents

4. Company Medical and First Aid Facilities

5. Industry/City Mutual Aid Arrangements

6. Company Repair and Restoration Group

7. Supplies Storage Facilities

8. Lists of:

   - Office Equipment

   - Supplies and Forms (Estimate)

9. List of Personnel, Addresses, and Telephone Numbers

- Database Administration Documentation

- Office Services Documentation

3.4   RESPONSIBILITIES OF OTHER GROUPS

A.   User Department Cooperation

User departments must accept a full role in the development of an EDP Disaster Recovery Plan and be prepared to cooperate with staff at various levels as the planning for it proceeds. Recognition that the EDP operation is a support organization, not an end in itself, is essential to the generation of realistic, cost-efficient contingency plans.

Because the EDP facility provides services, some of which are vital to the organization, senior user management should realize the critical nature of the dependence on contingency plans. Such plans serve to keep within tolerable limits the consequences of loss or damage to EDP resources. Economic feasibility of contingency plans requires careful analysis of decisions as to what user functions are deferable, and for how long. The costs of these deferrals should be established by the users.

It is impossible for such decisions to be reached entirely within the EDP organization. EDP management is not usually in a position to assess accurately the relative importance of all the work done for the supported areas. Further, the relative cost of the continued support of each, in the face of adversity, may vary quite widely. For these reasons, it is appropriate and important that senior user management provide direction and support for disaster recovery planning to provide essential functions following any disruption of the EDP facilities. They must also assign knowledgeable individuals to work on details with the team throughout the planning and testing process.

B.   Internal Audit Staff Involvement

Internal Audit staff have a critical role to play in disaster recovery planning. They must be intimately involved throughout the process, through to the final testing and maintenance.

Normally, Internal Audit will not be in charge of producing the plan because their prime function is to review it and comment on its adequacy. They should be involved at the earliest stages, however, to inform the team as to what administrative and accounting controls must be installed to give adequate internal control during a security event.

It must be recognized that adequate controls are more important during a disaster than at any other time. During normal operations, there is generally sufficient backup information available. If an application needs to be rerun, the data is probably still in existence, and the audit trail can be retraced and kept intact. During a disaster, however, input data may well have been lost, and it could even be unclear as to exactly when the event occurred during the processing. Audit trail programs and backup and recovery operations must take this problem into consideration. A critical disaster could even be caused by an employee to cover serious errors, losses, or a defalcation. This should be kept in mind and guarded against.

Among the recognized management objectives for which internal control is relevant are:

- Maximization of profitability and minimization of cost.

- Ensuring that management's policies and procedures are properly discharged.

- Ensuring that employees function within their scope of authority.

- Ensuring the timely preparation of reports, reconciliations, reviews, and other procedures.

- Provision for proper documentation procedures to help fix accountability and to substantiate transaction processing.

- Assurance of reliability and consistency of accounting records.

- Assurance of prevention, detection, and correction of errors and irregularities.

- Provision of adequate security over assets including vital information.

- Discharge of statutory and regulatory agency responsibilities.

These objectives are all well-described and developed in the FTP Technical Library publication "Internal Controls, Volume I, Design, Maintenance, and Assessment."

Discussions should be held with Internal Audit as to what part they should best play in the planning, when their input is appropriate, and when they should review the plan.

C. Involvement of Other Organizational Departments

An EDP Disaster Recovery Plan should be reviewed with nearly all other departments in the organization because they will either have a direct interest in the outcome (the user departments) or they have been assigned responsibilities which will include aspects of the plan. Such departments are:

- **Security Department:** They will normally have security and disaster recovery plans for the organization as a whole, which should be tied in carefully to the EDP plans. Any Fire Alarm Response plans, for example, will normally take precedence over all other plans because of the concern for safety of the employees.

- **Finance Department:** They will probably be one of the largest users of EDP service, and, hence, will be well represented in the planning.

- **Legal Department:** They should be asked what the legal aspects of handling a disaster are, including moves to other sites. They should also be asked to give management an opinion as to the applicability of the Foreign Corrupt Practices Act of 1977.

- **Audit Department:** The necessary involvement of Internal Audit was outlined above. They should also be asked at what stage the External Auditors should be brought in for discussion.

- **Medical Department:** It should be made clear to all EDP personnel that personnel safety is paramount during a disaster. The Medical Department may wish to discuss the effects of Halon and CO_2, and the possible dangers from electricity in the EDP facility. They should be asked how to handle medical problems at the backup sites.

- **Public Relations Department:** No one should discuss any EDP disasters with outsiders or the press without first consulting the Public Relations people. They will be responsible for any release of information outside the organization.

- **Labor Relations Department:** In union situations, there may be a number of restrictions on how the emergency backup operations can be handled and the number of staff that is required at the various sites. Rushing between installations, and changing people's commute patterns, can affect them profoundly. Even in non-union situations, the disaster plan should be discussed with Labor Relations.

- **Transportation Department:** They will be a key factor in moving people and equipment, setting up deliveries of supplies in new patterns, and providing shuttle-bus service between the sites.

- **Personnel Department:** All aspects of the duties in the plan should be discussed with them. Eager planners can easily over-extend their authority in the handling and assigning of people. Personnel will be particularly interested in what types of "calling-tree" lists will be drawn up and readily available for people to peruse. There may be restrictions on what can be printed and widely distributed.

- **Engineering Department:** They will normally have had a part in the design of the facilities, the environmental controls, and the fire protection system. Much free advice is available to EDP people on EDP facility design, but it should all be cleared with the Engineering Department. They may also be the best source of information as to available backup sites and how they could be prepared.

- **Buildings Department:** It is normally their responsibility to keep the buildings operating smoothly. Since they work with the whole organization, EDP should discuss the plans with them to see if there are any unavailable services or actions being taken which could damage other departments.

D.   Use of Consultants or Staff

EDP disaster recovery planning is no different from the many other technology-intensive projects that confront EDP management. These are two options: speed up the process by using consultants; or train in-house personnel, go through the learning curve, and hopefully benefit from the knowledge retained in-house. The advantages of using consultants are usually:

- Past Experience

- Rapid Start

- Comparison with Other Installations

- Previously Prepared Plan Details

- Objective Viewpoint

The advantages of using in-house personnel are:

- Rapid Training and Development in the Area

- Retention of Knowledge in the Organization

- Intimate Knowledge of many Details

- The Coordinator knows all Aspects of the Plan

The decision will be individual to each organization. Many organizations prefer a combination approach.

3.5   ORGANIZATION FOR INITIAL RESPONSE

The organization and procedures for the initial response to a disaster should be separate and distinct from the organization and activities of the Disaster Recovery Teams. The Initial Response procedures should be in the front of the Disaster Recovery procedures. They should be simple and clearly understood by the staff. They should also include a list of key management people to call, and the actions they will take.

When the night watchman, a security guard, a computer operator, or anyone else, detects an apparent disastrous security event, they should know rapidly which management personnel to call, in which order. They should be able to refer to a posted list.

A.   Initial Response Management Team

The Initial Response Management Team should not necessarily consist of senior EDP management, although those people will be called also. It is generally most advantageous to gather a team consisting of managers in at least the following areas:

- EDP Operations

- Systems Programming

- Applications Systems (Covering the Most Critical Systems)

Their home telephone numbers, plus the numbers of alternates in case they are not available at the time they are called, should be clearly listed in the Disaster Recovery Procedures. If any one of them gets called, he should try to affirm that the others have also been called. They should then proceed to the site of the disaster as rapidly as possible. Once they have arrived, they should in no way interfere with any Fire Department activity or Bomb Disposal activity.

The purpose of the Initial Response Management Team is to make an evaluation of which part of the Disaster Recovery Procedures to put into action, confirm their findings with EDP management, and start any necessary actions.

B.   Disaster Recovery Evaluation

The Initial Response Management Team will, together, have a very broad understanding of all the EDP operations and procedures. They will be able to make an accurate technical estimate of the extent of the damages and the backup requirements immediately needed. They will know what responses to the event will be most advantageous.

Having agreed among themselves as to the best technical course of action, they will inform senior EDP management of what has happened, and give them the agreed recommendations. In all likelihood, senior EDP management will have arrived on the scene by this time. Note that most disasters occur at night or on weekends because there are fewer people around to observe and handle incipient incidents than there are during the day. A small wastebasket fire that could be doused with a pot of coffee in the morning working hours could well get out of hand and destroy part of a building at night. Thus, this disaster recovery evaluation will likely take place during off hours.

If the senior EDP management agrees with the Initial Response Team's evaluation, then they will give the signal to activate the recovery plans. If it is a small disaster, they may take action immediately. If it is a larger disaster, and the results will affect other departments, they will probably not take major actions until they have called and consulted with some senior officers of the organization. This will, of course, depend on circumstances. If it is a large fire, most other managers in the organization will already have been alerted. If the event is confined to the EDP area, however, there may not be general knowledge of it in the first hours, even though it has the potential for affecting all business operations.

C.   Activation of EDP Disaster Recovery Teams

As soon as the Initial Response Team's recommendations have been accepted or modified, and management has received necessary clearances and started the recovery plan in operation, the "phone trees" will start to activate all the EDP Disaster Recovery Teams.

It is likely that the Initial Response Team will include leaders of specific Disaster Recovery Teams, so little time should be lost in getting action started. If it is on a weekend or late at night, it could well be that many people are unavailable on the first calls. Usually, however, sufficient people to start the action plan can arrive quickly. Organizations with "beeper" systems that can put out an automatic general alarm message to all beepers can get very rapid response.

Once the EDP Disaster Recovery Teams are activated and informed of the course of action to take, they will be operating independently in parallel. A great deal of work can be accomplished in a short time if most people know their assigned tasks. Of course, they will all be regularly reporting to EDP senior management, who will coordinate the planned actions.

There should be a Disaster Recovery Control Center where EDP management will be located to issue orders and take reports. It is better located in a conference room near the original site rather than near the backup site. The reason is that it will be simpler near the original site to keep in contact with all other departments in the organization. In addition, EDP's own staff members, who had not heard of the disaster or orders, would probably come by that way first. If such a Control Center is planned and used, the greatest need is several telephones. These should always be located close together so that all management participants are informed of what the others are saying and doing. It is easier to have a conversation overheard than it is to repeat it. In preparing for disaster recovery, several phone lines with jacks could be installed in an appropriate room.

The number of Disaster Recovery Teams to be planned and given assignments will naturally depend on the size of the organization and the complexity of the operations. **Figure 3-2, Disaster Recovery Teams,** gives examples of how teams may be organized for different sized companies. Clearly, the organization of the teams must be selected by the classical approach of reasonable "span of control." No one should have more than five people reporting to them. A normal management pyramid structure can go to many levels. In an emergency, however, the fewer levels, the better to get the message across rapidly.

Figure 3-2

EDP DISASTER RECOVERY TEAMS

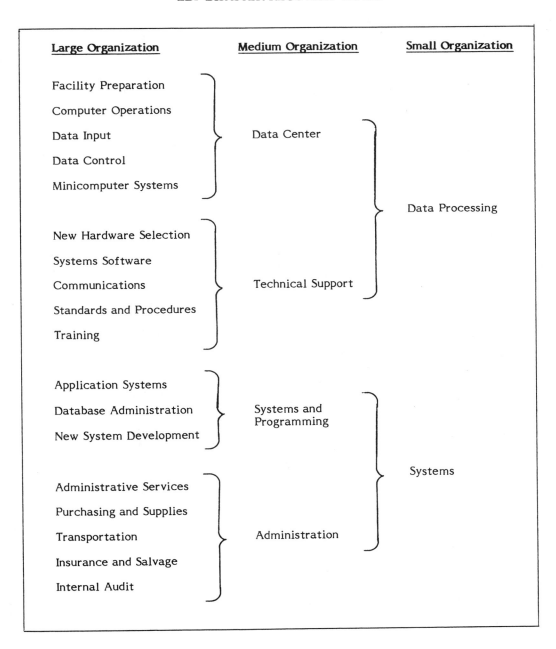

SECTION 4

REQUIREMENTS AND STRATEGY DECISIONS

SECTION OVERVIEW

This section discusses the types of disaster which should be considered in planning, and the purpose of a Key Disaster Scenario. It also aids in planning of the critical resources and applications which must be given priority in the plan.

A number of alternative recovery strategies are discussed, with their advantages and disadvantages, and the types of contracts that may be needed. The selection and development of a combination strategy is suggested.

Procedures are outlined for making a cost/benefit analysis to justify the planning and preparations. Costs of possible losses and costs of measures for recovery are discussed. Approaches to the identification of risks are included.

4.1 OBJECTIVES, ASSUMPTIONS, AND DEFINITIONS

It was pointed out in Section 3, Personnel Participation in the Plan, that the first task of the EDP Disaster Recovery Planning Team is to develop a Disaster Recovery Project Plan to outline, estimate the time and cost, and get management approvals for the planning. This may be an initial, short-term, high-impact plan. Later, it may be a full disaster recovery plan for all of Information Services. The questions then arise:

- What sorts of disaster are we talking about?

- What are, realistically, the critical resources and applications?

- What sorts of strategies are available?

- What are the possible losses and the costs for recovery measures?

The Recovery Planning Team must develop initial answers to such questions quickly so that management will understand the worth of the project and know how much effort to put into it. The team's study and analysis will then lead to more accurate statements and more reasonable estimates, and management will then be able to decide on further funding and implementation of the project. It is most difficult to guess what is needed without going through a detailed analysis. Thus, the first step in the preparation of the plan is to make an initial statement of the objectives, assumptions, and definitions.

A. Objectives:

The objectives may be stated in a variety of ways, depending on the organization:

- To maintain customer service at an acceptable level.

- To keep operations running smoothly with less than an "X" hour break in computer services.

- To meet all government requirements for service.

- To assure management that the Foreign Corrupt Practices Act requirements have been met.

- To handle an interruption and change of computers with a satisfactory audit trail.

The objectives are statements of management intent for the smooth operation and profitability of the organization.

B.   Assumptions:

Preliminary assumptions should then be developed by the team. The assumptions should include any guidelines that management has given the team to start the project, and any initial boundaries for the project that the team deems appropriate. Some examples of assumptions and boundaries would be:

- The Disaster Recovery Procedures will include all aspects of Information Services operations, including Purchasing and Stores, Mailroom and Distribution, and all on-line terminal areas.

- The intent will be, in the event of a disaster, to restore the key financial production applications within 24 hours, a selected group of applications within 7 days, and a large percentage of the applications within 20 days. (These requirements will be examined in detail in the study.)

- The industry is considered as low-risk, and the operation is in an average-risk area. Special considerations for floods, earthquakes, and riots are not required.

- The costs of any disaster recovery preparations will be funded as required by management and will not be part of the normal operating budget of Information Services.

- The precautions will be complementary to existing Fire and Emergency Procedures and will be of lower priority.

- Full risk analysis calculations are only required for a selected list of critical applications, the requirements of which will be adequate justification for the project.

The list of assumptions will, naturally, be given to and discussed with management as soon as possible.

C.   Definitions:

It is best to prepare a rough draft of the definitions of the terms that will be used, the concept of "disaster," and the areas under consideration that are assumed in the disaster recovery study. The definitions should be written for clarification to management and should, therefore, be straightforward and not technical.

4.2   TYPES OF DISASTER TO CONSIDER

No reasonable planning can be done without first reaching an agreement within the organization as to what types of disaster could realistically affect the operation, and which are the most probable. This decision will set the first major assumption to be made in creating the plan. It will also be fundamental to deciding the types of security measures that should be installed. It will be the starting point in estimating the losses to be expected from disaster occurrences and the costs of measures to protect against those losses.

TYPES OF DISASTER

The various types of disaster to consider include:

A. Natural Disasters:

Floods	Earthquakes
Winter Storms	Hurricanes

B. Man-Made Disasters:

Fires	Burst Pipes
Accidents	Building Collapse
Thefts	Bomb Threats
Willful Destruction	Plane Crash
Sabotage	

C. Political Disasters:

Riots and Civil Disturbances	Strikes
War	Nuclear Attack

This list should be considered by the management involved, and the necessary response should be agreed upon. It will depend upon the area of operation of the organization, the location of EDP equipment, and the location of information needs. For example, if the organization's operations are located in a limited geographic area, its disaster response requirements will be quite different than those for national operation. A disaster could realistically wipe out the need of EDP operations if it destroyed most of the organization's operations in a limited area. Similarly, some groups will have more concern with earthquakes or hurricanes than will others.

The most likely threats should receive the most attention. These disasters may be localized, and preparation for them will be the direct responsibility of Information Services management. Disasters, such as major building fires or hurricanes, are normally the responsibility of other groups in the company as they are generally too extensive for consideration by Information Services people only. Concern for the general organization operations will then be overriding. The same procedures to back up the EDP facilities should apply, but there will be less concern with the organization's cash flow from the EDP point of view, and far more concern with the protection of the people and the maintenance of overall organization services.

If an organization is widespread, there is considerable incentive to maintain a distant (at least 100 miles) backup site. If an organization is in a narrow geographic area, the backup site could be much closer. In either case, the maintenance of vital records must be in a secure place, regardless of geography. The concept of disaster backup sites for vital records is relatively independent of backup operations sites.

4.2.1   MOST PROBABLE DISASTER OCCURRENCES

Having agreed on the types of disaster to consider, the study team involved, and management, should analyze the most probable disaster occurrences. If this list is of reasonable length, or if the effects of the occurrences will be different, and are readily grouped, a Disaster Recovery Scenario could be written for each type of occurrence, and plans laid for each scenario.

A practical approach, however, is to pick from the list the type of disaster that would be of greatest concern to the Information Services area. This can be considered in developing the Key Disaster Scenario. Detailed plans could then be laid for it. All other incidents would be considered either subsets of the plan, and decisions could be made at the time as to what parts of the plan would be used, or they could be extensions of it, and the full plan would be used together with other organization activities.

Normally, the Key Disaster Scenario will focus on an occurrence involving the computer room, or nearby areas of the EDP facility. This threat would be of particular concern, because it could concentrate in the EDP facility area and not physically affect the rest of the organization. If Information Services is an integral part of the organization's operations, the effect on financial control and cash flow could be disastrous. A sustained shutdown of the EDP facility, while the rest of the organization is trying to operate normally, would be most serious for Information Services management. The Key Disaster Scenario, and the disaster recovery procedures, should be designed especially to meet this threat.

There are five types of disaster to which Information Services operations could generally be vulnerable. This is an arbitrary list which should be modified by the Team. In order of their probability, they are:

a.   **Damage to Individual Terminal Areas**

Fire, water damage, bomb threat, or other destruction in a localized situation in a terminal area is the most probable type of disaster to occur. This could be from common causes, such as electric wiring faults or waste basket burning. It would require some readjustment of the communications, and the establishment of new terminal facilities, depending upon the priority of the operations involved.

b.   **Localized Damage in Information Services Offices**

Similiar types of disaster to the above become more critical when they occur in the systems, programming, key input, or support services areas of Information Services. It is likely that such disaster could affect production schedules, systems development work, or general information distribution. Such incidents could also affect a number of different users at the same time, and records could be destroyed that are difficult to replace.

c.   **Damage to the EDP Facilities Area**

Substantial fire, water leak, or bomb threat to areas adjacent to the computer room represent the most likely serious problems to affect Information Services' continued operation. The location of the disaster could be more important than the size of the disaster in this case. A relatively small security event could cripple the whole EDP facility. Damage of this type is uniquely the problem of Information Services management, and is normally selected as the Key Disaster Scenario. Although the most likely problem may be a small electrical fire in a contained area, the effect of it could extend to all users of the computer services, and the response may have to be complete relocation of the computer operation.

d.   **Substantial Damage to the Organization's Offices**

Major fire, major flood from burst pipes, or major bomb or riot threat affecting a large part of the Organization's offices may affect the EDP facilities simultaneously. In this case there may be little salvageable equipment or space throughout the area. Organization operational problems would take precedence, but it would be up to Information Services to recover their operations simultaneously. The Key Disaster Scenario should still be the basis of the activities to be undertaken, even though it would probably have a serious effect on the EDP plans.

e.   **Regional Damage in a Broad Area**

Extremely heavy storms, floods, hurricanes, or acts of war could affect a broad part of the operating area of the organization. There could be widespread loss of power and telephone lines, disrupted public transportation, and substantial difficulty for employees in reporting to work. If this damage covered most of the operating area of the organization, then Information Services would simply follow overall priorities, and apply its Key Disaster Scenario when it became possible to do so. If this damage was regional, and the organization is national, then the Disaster Recovery Plan would have to include preparations for a major move of all operations to a distant site. Hopefully, that site and its alternates would have been selected, prepared, and planned for in advance of the disaster recovery.

The Key Disaster Scenario for most companies need not be concerned with acts of war, such as nuclear bombing, widespread hurricane damage and flooding, or particularly severe winter storms. Such disasters will have such an overriding effect on the company's general operations, that EDP recovery will be a minor part of the problems facing management. In such cases, for most companies, Information Services management will probably be able to follow their Key Disaster Scenario after the initial stabilization of the overall situation.

There are a variety of types of possible disaster that can be unique to an industry or a section of the country. These should be considered by the study team. Each organization must decide their threats of greatest concern, and how incidents will be handled with at least one Key Disaster Scenario. Particular attention must obviously be paid to the EDP facilities area. Any Information Service disaster plan must be subordinate to emergency fire alarm procedures, or bomb threat procedures, as the safety of personnel must be of utmost concern.

4.3   KEY DISASTER SCENARIO

The greatest probability of any disaster (fire, water, bomb, etc.) striking Information Services will be that a localized security event will affect one or more user areas. This would cause a need for a small group to move temporarily, and for terminals to be moved and connected in new locations. In such cases, the Emergency Management Team will meet and decide what pieces of the EDP Disaster Recovery Plan to put into effect. They will not call everyone in to participate, but only the personnel directly affected. No specific preparations need be made in advance for such a scenario, because it will be a subset of the Key Disaster Scenario, and handled accordingly. There is a great variety of occurrences possible in such a localized disaster, and it would be fruitless to try to prepare scenarios for each of them.

There is a critical disaster scenario, however, which will be called the Key Disaster Scenario. Such a disaster could have a marked effect on the company's operations and profits, and it is necessary that Information Services make preparations in advance for it to minimize its impact. The Key Disaster Scenario will normally call for the full implementation of the Disaster Recovery Plan.

The disaster which triggers the Key Disaster Scenario will likely be a fire, flood, or explosion that occurs in the vicinity of the main computer room, particularly near the communications equipment and lines or the power supply. It could be on another floor, with the resulting water and smoke damage impinging on the computer room.

The Key Disaster Scenario does not necessarily start with a large and impressive security event. A small, localized fire or flood can easily knock out a large computer center. The problem that faces Information Services management is that few other people in the organization may even be aware that such an event has occurred, yet all their computer services have suddenly been cut off.

The Recovery Planning Team should examine the areas involved, discuss with others the types of problems that the organization has experienced or which may occur, then outline their opinion of the Key Disaster Scenario to keep the plans in perspective, and to make management aware of what they are working to alleviate.

A typical Key Disaster Scenario, in brief outline, may be:

- A security event occurs in an area close to the main computer room at midnight on a Friday. (Note that the majority of disasters which cause great damage occur at night or on weekends. When there is an incipient fire, leak, or break-in during working hours, the chances are good that it will be handled before it becomes disastrous.)

- A night operator or a security guard detects the event, and rings the alarm. Local Fire and Police departments arrive on the scene.

- The person who rang the alarm calls the organization's security or building manager, in accordance with the posted instructions in the guard room.

- A person who knows the existence of the EDP Disaster Recovery Plan calls one or more of the Emergency Management Team. They, in turn, call the responsible Information Services manager.

- The Emergency Management Team gathers at the site as rapidly as possible and determines what has happened, and what has already been done by the Fire Department and others. They make their preliminary estimates in accordance with the Disaster Recovery Procedures, and discuss the possibilities with Information Services management.

- A decision is made on the extent of the operational needs, the "phone trees" are started, and the Disaster Recovery Plan is put into effect.

The initial security event may well have caused:

- Destruction of the communications controller and an undetermined number of telephone or coax lines.

- Undetermined damage to the main computer system, with water on the floor beneath the computer room.

- Water and smoke damage to the Data Input and Data Control areas, and smoke damage to a large part of the programmers' offices.

- Water damage to the power supply in the basement below.

The study team should consider what likely damage could readily occur to the whole Information Services area if fire equipment and hoses were brought in to get the fire under control anywhere near the computer room.

It will be sufficient for many organizations to have a single Key Disaster Scenario, base all their plans around it, and count on the Emergency Management Team and the Information Services senior managers to select and handle the response actions. Larger organizations, and those with different sized data centers, however, may well wish to plan on from two to five scenarios, and lay out the details for all of them. This approach could certainly be satisfactory, but it must be remembered that it will be much more expensive to create, and more difficult to keep updated in satisfactory detail.

4.4   ASSESSMENT OF RESOURCE REQUIREMENTS

4.4.1   MINIMUM RECOVERY PROCEDURES REQUIRED

The prompt recovery of an EDP facility from a loss of capability depends on the availability of a number of resources. The particular resources to be planned for will depend on the most probable disaster occurrences to be expected. Some resources will be essential to reestablish operations. The minimum recovery procedures to be developed must include the continuing availability of those resources. Procedures must be in place which rapidly recognize the loss of such critical resources. There are two categories of resource dependence which must be considered. These are:

1.   Resources under the direct control of EDP management. This will include the preservation of vital records and the means of running mandatory and necessary programs.

2.   Resources under the control of other groups. When resources are under the control of persons outside the EDP area, firm commitments must be obtained to operate them in the context of the Disaster Recovery Plan. Priorities and recovery procedures must be agreed upon to have a comprehensive plan that fits well together. Rehearsals and tests must include these resources together with those in EDP. Recovery procedures must be uniform.

The continuation of a large percentage of the EDP operations at an alternate site immediately after a disruption is rarely logistically, technically, or economically feasible. It is seldom essential. The tasks performed by an EDP facility are not all of equal importance. This must be reflected in the recovery procedures. The relative importance of the various functions must be analyzed, and the procedures designed to step through the various functions in priority order.

In addition, the Disaster Recovery Procedures must be tailored specifically to the organization using them. Few EDP operations are so similiar in equipment configuration, applications, environment, and relative criticality of functions, that a general-purpose recovery plan can be drawn up and used. Even in large organizations with multiple distributed operation centers that are designed identically, the personnel involved, their home phone numbers, and their specific instructions will vary. Of course, an organization can produce a uniform, fill-in-the-blanks plan for its internal units. In this manual, therefore, the approach is to present a guideline for preparing a specific plan which will then be suitable to the special needs of each EDP facility.

46

However, for any disaster recovery plan, regardless of size or scope of operations, at a minimum, the recovery procedures should address these three elements:

1. **Emergency Response Procedures:**

   Emergency response procedures to document the appropriate emergency response to a fire, flood, civil disorder, natural disaster, bomb threat or any other incident or activity in order to protect lives, limit damage, and minimize the impact on data processing operations.

2. **Backup Operations Procedures:**

   Backup Operations procedures to ensure that essential data processing operational tasks can be conducted after disruption to the primary data processing facility. Arrangements should be made for a backup capability, including the needed files, programs, paper stocks and preprinted forms, etc., to operate the essential systems functions in the event of a total failure.

3. **Recovery Actions Procedures:**

   Recovery actions procedures to facilitate the rapid restoration of a data processing facility following physical destruction, major damage, or loss of data.

In addition, it is a requirement that disaster recovery procedures be tested on a recurring basis, and modified as changes in the data processing facility workload dictate. Critical applications should be operated on the backup system to ensure that it can properly process them.

4.4.2   APPLICATION SYSTEMS REQUIREMENTS

Application Systems requirements must be determined individually and in detail before any priorities are set and assessments are made for the disaster recovery planning. The EDP Disaster Recovery Planning Team must discuss individually, with each Systems Analysis group, the details of each application system and their view of its priority. Discussions must then be held with the user contacts to get their views of the availability requirements and the priorities of the system. Finally, management must review the findings and determine the priorities and requirements that will be planned for and funded.

Even if management calls for creating an initial high-impact, short-term recovery plan, the requirements of all operating application systems should be at least briefly reviewed:

- To be sure that no critical applications are omitted.

- To establish a full application systems priority listing which can be reviewed by management.

a. **Application System Service Availability Requirements:**

For the purposes of discussion and analysis, the team can use **Figure 4-1, Application System Service Availability Requirements** to get a first understanding of what the disaster recovery needs will be. For large application systems, groups of programs may be used to subdivide the entries. Rough estimates are acceptable on the first review of the application. The columns of Figure 4-1 are:

Application Systems: Names of systems, groups of programs, or individual programs, as is reasonable.

Report Frequency: For batch reports. Response time for on-line.

On-Line or Batch: If both, separate the line entries.

Areas of Exposure: Legal requirements, financial, customer service, public relations, etc.

Unacceptable Period of Loss of Availability: Start with the user's statements about acceptability of any disruption. Discuss later.

Potential Losses: Give initial estimates for hour, day, week, and month, if applicable. If a risk analysis is made, these numbers will be refined for specific systems.

Other Considerations: Mention Foreign Corrupt Practices Act, if applicable, and any senior management directives.

It will be useful to develop an Application System Service Availability Requirements form for nearly all application systems, even those of low priority in the first analysis. Clearly, low priority systems need not have the same level of analysis in detail as the higher priority systems.

b. **Application Systems Priority:**

After all application systems have been identified and some information has been gathered about them, the team should discuss their priority with more senior management. All application systems in each group or division of the organization should then be ranked in priority sequence according to the desires of the management of that group or division. **Figure 4-2, Application Systems Priority,** may be used for this ranking.

Figure 4-1

APPLICATION SYSTEM SERVICE AVAILABILITY REQUIREMENTS

Group or Division _____

Application System	Report Frequency	On-Line or Batch	Areas of Exposure	Unacceptable Period of Loss Of Availability	Potential Losses	Other Considerations

Figure 4-2

APPLICATION SYSTEMS PRIORITY

Group or Division _____

Priority	Application System	Systems Contact	User Contact	Basic Processing Reqmts.	Report Frequency	Minimum Terminal Reqmts.	New Development?	Comments
Top Five								
1								
2								
3								
4								
5								
Approx.								
6								
7								
8								
Etc.								

It is not necessarily simple to assign a rank order or priority to all systems, so the effort should be put into ranking the "Top Five" (or other number as seems reasonable) and then giving only an approximate priority to the remainder. After the application system priorities have been agreed upon in each group or division, the team must then discuss with senior management how to assign relative priorities to the different groups so that an overall priority list can be developed. This is usually not difficult as it is fairly obvious which are the top priority systems in an organization. The columns of Figure 4-2 are:

Priority: Firm listing of the "Top Five" as discussed and approximate listing of the remainder.

Application System: Name of system or groups of programs within a system.

Systems Contact: Name of lead systems analyst for the application system.

User Contact: Names of working systems contact, plus user manager involved with the system operation.

Basic Processing Requirements: Computer, memory used, and the operating system used.

Report Frequency: For principal reports. Note if on-line for reports, data entry, or both.

Minimum Terminal Requirements: The type of terminals and the fewest number of them that would be needed in disaster recovery.

New Development: Note if any substantial modification or development is presently being undertaken on the system.

Comments: Management requirements, special requirements, etc.

This form should be filled out carefully for the "Top Five" systems or any with special considerations. Less information is needed for the other systems.

c. **Audit Control Requirements:**

The Audit Control requirements of critical application systems at the time of a disaster are more complex and may be more difficult to handle than the basic backup and recovery of the system. The team should consult with Internal Audit personnel about these requirements and pay particular attention to them. It is not unreasonable to suspect that the cause of a disaster could be the cover-up of a defalcation or the poor operation of a system.

An excellent analysis of the Environmental Control Objectives and the Application Control Objectives for the EDP systems is presented in "Internal Controls, Volume I: Design, Maintenance, and Assessment," published by the FTP Technical Library. Internal Auditors and systems personnel can use this and its companion, "Volume II: Control Descriptions." A brief summary of the Application Control Objectives described in these manuals is given in **Figure 4-3, Application Control Objectives.**

4.4.3   DATA AND SOFTWARE REQUIREMENTS

a.   Data File Requirements:

Data files are subject to a number of vulnerabilities which should be examined in detail by the team during the risk analysis and in considering how to handle the backup and recovery. Separate consideration must be given to the data in the computer operating system, the data residing in miscellaneous files around the facility, and the data that is secured in backup storage.

An accidental destruction of data can cause a serious disruption of data processing if replacement data are not promptly available. It is mandatory to define the responsibility of individuals who will analyze the protection and recovery of data resources and recommend actions to protect them. This will include:

- What happens if some of the source data is destroyed?

- What happens if an incident disrupts a computer in the middle of processing?

- What types of backup files must be routinely created?

- How many generations of backup files are needed to be sure there is rapid, accurate recovery?

- How much information should be put in geographically remote vital records storage facilities?

Most of the data considerations will have been adequately analyzed if the organization is operating under a database system and if there are competent database administration personnel. Such problems as listed above are obvious to them and will have already been considered. This should be ascertained, however.

There can be serious problems involved with the backup and recovery of on-line operations unless considerable thought has gone into the logging of data input and the establishment of good audit trails. These problems should have been addressed in the original system analysis but should be reviewed in the disaster recovery study.

Figure 4-3

APPLICATION CONTROL OBJECTIVES

1. **Accurate Data**

   Accurate data implies the need for correction of inaccuracies associated with data preparation, conversion to machine-readable format, processing by the computer, or in the output preparation and delivery processes. It also implies the retention of data control capabilities during a security event.

2. **Complete Data**

   Completeness of processed data requires that data is not lost during preparation, in transit to the computer, during processing, between interrelated computer systems, and/or in transit to users of that data. It also implies the retention of the audit trail of the data through the disaster recovery operations.

3. **Timely Data**

   The timely processing of data ensures that management has the necessary information to take action in time to avoid avoidable losses. The discussions on priority should determine the recovery actions required to maintain the necessary timeliness.

4. **Authorized Data**

   Controls should ensure that any unauthorized data is detected prior to and during processing. This can be sensitive during a disaster recovery.

5. **Processed According to GAAP**

   Financial data should be processed in accordance with Generally Accepted Accounting Procedures. Controls should assure these procedures are followed even through a security event.

6. **Compliance with Organization's Policies and Procedures**

   Organization policies and procedures for handling transaction data should be reviewed by the team. Controls should assure these policies are followed.

7. **Compliance with Laws and Regulations**

   The laws and regulations of regulatory agencies are normally the driving force behind establishing a Disaster Recovery Plan. Controls should ensure that the laws and regulations are followed, therefore.

8. **Adequate Supporting Evidence**

   Sufficient evidence to reconstruct transactions and pinpoint accountability for processing should enable the tracing from source documents to control totals, and from the control totals back to the supporting transactions. The keeping of a trail of evidence through a disaster could be difficult. Responsible users must be involved in maintaining such ability.

Extracted from: "Internal Controls, Volume I: Design, Maintenance, and Assessment" FTP Technical Library, 492 Old Town Road, Port Jefferson Station, New York 11776

The detailed problems of the security and backup of data are inherent to systems design and beyond the scope of this discussion. However, all data on which a backup and recovery operation is dependent must be adequately recorded and maintained in current condition and backup copies be adequately secured. It is generally the responsibility of systems personnel to ensure the security of machine-readable data. It is the responsibility of the users to keep records of their input and sufficient backup information to recover from a disaster.

If a database management system, or even just a data dictionary, has been fully and properly implemented, and sufficient copies are maintained in a current and physically safe condition, most contingency requirements for data can be readily met. It will not be necessary to describe the system again in the recovery plan.

b. **Software Requirements:**

Systems software and application programs are a special case of data handling. In fact, most backup tapes simply group all machine-readable data together. In time of emergency, it is then the problem of Systems Programming to strip out the various meaningful groups of information.

Software programs tend to have greater stability than does data, but they are sufficiently subject to change that care must be exercised that fully current versions, and all documentation, are sufficiently protected.

Application programs can be particularly vulnerable in EDP operations if there is not careful management attention to the use of development disciplines and change control. Formalized program management procedures are necessary to be assured that programs can be rapidly backed up. If an author/programmer is in any way needed to keep normal operations going, it will be difficult to have a workable contingency plan.

One of the critical disaster recovery preparations that is required is to work out formal agreements with the vendors of any licensed program packages that are used. The copying of these is generally forbidden in the contract, so it is up to the vendor to maintain the ready availability of replacement copies. They should be prepared to state from where replacement copies will be shipped, how soon they could be expected after a security event, and whether they will have personnel available to give support to the recovery process.

4.1.4   VITAL RECORDS REQUIREMENTS AND RECORDS RETENTION ANALYSIS

Vital Records are those necessary to ensure the survival of a business. It is important that vital records be given maximum protection from every possible disaster because the information contained in those records may be the single, most valuable asset of the organization. Some vital records are processing and trade secrets, drawings, formulas, and so on. Other vital records are in the accounting, operating, and engineering information that is resident on computer media.

Normally, less than two percent of a company's records can be described as vital unless the organization primarily deals with data, such as banking or insurance. In most organizations, a Records Manager, or some other responsible person, has already determined which records are vital and has established a vital records protection program. It is helpful to EDP if this program has included the establishment of a remote, safe storage facility which can be used to store necessary backup tapes and documentation.

In a modern data processing operation, the handling of the records that have been determined as "vital" is generally completely interwoven with the handling of the records that are considered critical for the operations of the mandatory and necessary application systems. The vital records will be classified as "mandatory," and the systems handling them will certainly be given high priority. EDP backup information on electronic media is seldom separated into vital and non-vital categories, however, as backup tapes and disks usually have full application systems on them ready to be stripped out as needed. Despite this fact, the team should be cognizant of which material is "vital" and which is not. They will normally have to assure the Records Manager or the Corporate Secretary that all vital records have been considered and identified and are being given adequate protection.

In general, the measures that are taken to assure the general efficiency of the computer and its use by the company, and to back up mandatory and necessary systems, are identical to those measures that should be taken to protect vital data processing operations. It is sufficient for the team to identify the vital records, then treat them in the "mandatory" class of backup and recovery handling.

<u>Records Retention Analysis</u> is related to vital records requirements because its prime legal use is for the vital records. It should be extended to all data processing records, however, because of its usefulness in keeping some control on the volume of retained data. There are three types of retention purposes. These are:

1. **Legal Retention:** The period of time required by such agencies as the IRS and the Interstate Commerce Commission. These required records become vital records.

2. **Processing Retention:** The period of time specified in the Operations Manual as necessary to restart the processing of that data in the event an error is detected subsequent to initial processing.

3. **Disaster Retention:** The storing of necessary data on a computer media that facilitates off-site storage on a cyclical basis sufficient to resume normal data processing activities in the event of a disaster at the computer site.

The EDP Disaster Recovery Project Team should be able to collect the above retention information from the Systems Analysts involved with the application systems. It should not need to be developed at the time of the study but should be known by those responsible for the systems. **Figure 4-4, Records Retention Periods,** is an example of such analysis.

Figure 4-4
(Page 1)

RECORDS RETENTION PERIODS

A. Records with Retention Periods Specified by Government Regulation

Type of Record	Retention Period (Yrs.)	Type of Record	Retention Period (Yrs.)
Accounting & Fiscal		**Purchasing & Procurement**	
Accounts Payable Invoices	3	Bids and Awards	3
Checks, Payroll	2	Purchase Orders & Reqs.	3
Checks, Voucher	3	**Security**	
Earnings Register	3	Employee Clearance Records	5
General Ledger Records	Permanent	Visitor Records	2
Labor Cost Records	3	**Taxation**	
Payroll Registers	3	Annuity and Other Plans	Permanent
Manufacturing		Dividend Register	Permanent
Bills and Material	3	Employee Taxes	4
Engineering & Specs. Records	20	Excise Reports	4
Stock Issuing Records	3	Inventory Reports	Permanent
Personnel		Depreciation Schedules	Permanent
Accident Reports & Claims	30	**Transportation**	
Changes and Terminations	5	Bills of Lading	2
Injury Frequency Records	Permanent	Freight Bills	3
Job Ratings	2	Freight Claims	2

Figure 4-4
(Page 2)

RECORDS RETENTION PERIODS

B. Typical Records with Retention Periods Fixed by Administrative Decision

Type of Record	Retention Period (Yrs.)	Type of Record	Retention Period (Yrs.)
Accounting & Fiscal		**Manufacturing**	
Accounts Payable Ledger	Permanent	Production Reports	3
Accounts Receivable Ledger	5	Work Orders	3
Bank Statements	3	**Personnel**	
Budgets	3	Attendance Records	7
Expense Reports	3	Employee Activity Files	3
Financial Statements, Cert.	Permanent	**Plant Records**	
P & L Statements	Permanent	Inventory Records	Permanent
Commission Reports	3	Maintenance Records	5
Corporate		**Taxation**	
Capital Stock Ledger	Permanent	Tax Bills & Statements	Permanent
Stock Transfer Records	Permanent	Tax Returns	Permanent

Note: The above Retention Periods are given as typical examples. In practice, an organization must determine its own Records Retention Periods.

4.4.5 HARDWARE AND COMMUNICATIONS REQUIREMENTS

a. Hardware Requirements:

Hardware resources are usually readily replaceable if the equipment is of recent manufacture and is produced in sufficient quantity for the manufacturer to have replacement devices ready to ship on short notice. The policy of most hardware manufacturers is that, in the event of a localized disaster, the customer will be moved to the front of the line for shipment of replacement units that are available. Some CPU's may require a larger, more modern replacement because the other is no longer in production. For other units, the vendor may ship one that they are using for demonstration. In any event, most hardware vendors are prepared to give the most rapid replacement service possible. Their engineers will normally work around the clock to bring up the needed system. There are some differences between various vendors, however, and agreements or understandings should be obtained well in advance of problems occurring. Only a few of the vendors will put detailed agreements in writing, but experience has shown that the great majority will put forth a "best effort" and will state in advance that they will do so.

Those EDP installations that have multiple-vendor mixed equipment, must be aware that each vendor will normally supply only replacements for their own equipment if the replacements are coming out of their delivery line. Otherwise, they could have legal difficulty with their other customers.

There are a number of hardware devices that may be quite difficult to replace rapidly in an emergency. These include:

- Equipment which has a complex array of optional features and has been effectively customized for the application. Complex communications controllers are an example.

- Equipment manufactured in small quantities or on demand. Large memory arrays are an example.

- Equipment which is application sensitive, such as check sorters.

- Equipment that is approaching, or may have reached, obsolescence, such as older versions of computers.

- Equipment manufactured by companies no longer in existence. The used equipment market should be searched for replacements.

The ease of replacement of hardware is usually a secondary consideration in disaster recovery planning because most manufacturers are attuned to giving emergency aid. At a very minimum, it still takes 24 to 48 hours to get replacement hardware, however, and it then has to be tested and brought up. Frequently, deliveries take several days.

Therefore, if there are functions that cannot wait a few days and need immediate backup access, the backup hardware to be used must be already in place and operating at an existing site. This could be your own equipment, agreements with others, or commercial installations. The actual details must be carefully arranged in this stage of the disaster recovery preparations.

The priorities established for the processing of functions on the backup facility must be based on a realistic assessment of hardware availability. The vendor should be asked to help in this assessment.

b. Communications Requirements:

The size and complexity of the communications network supporting an EDP facility is a major factor in contingency planning. The dependency of time-critical functions must be understood in detail before steps can be planned to provide backup and recovery. The Telephone Company normally responds very rapidly in restoring communications lines. The problem lies in restoring sufficient numbers of terminals, modems, controllers, etc., and in adjusting the systems software to recognize the new configuration from a new computer and a new location. It may be necessary to change local operation to remote and vice versa. Clearly, the systems programming problems are considerable and require careful planning if rapid recovery is a necessity.

Common carriers have available the means to switch leased telephone lines under remote customer control from the initial termination to alternate sites. The switch, the controllers, and the lines are all tariffed separately and may even be supplied by separate vendors. The complications are obvious, but the rapid switching of many lines may be economically feasible if the organization's dependency on them is great. This must all be reviewed in the preparatory analysis. If there is careful planning, the greatest problem will still be in the development of the required systems software to exactly meet the previously unused configuration.

Clearly, if it is important enough, the capability must be developed to route all communications to each of two (or more) sites. With this alternative, there can be a rapid changeover from a damaged site to the backup. The economic feasibility and the time dependencies must be analyzed carefully to determine the necessary approach to communications backup.

4.4.6   OTHER RESOURCE REQUIREMENTS

a. Personnel Requirements:

Personnel are the most critical resources of any EDP organization. Recovery from damaging losses is highly dependent on the availability and participation of knowledgeable, experienced personnel. People provide the flexibility, availability, and versatility needed to meet an unexpected situation and to adapt the previously made plans to the situation as it actually exists. It is, therefore, necessary that all personnel who are to be involved in a recovery plan have studied the plan, have been trained in its execution, and have been given an opportunity to suggest changes and additions.

People can be expected to innovate, perform unfamiliar tasks, work under stress, and work long hours if they are doing and feel that they are a part of the plan. For a successful recovery operation, belief in the inherent importance of the organization's mission must have been instilled previously to motivate the staff to carry out the work under stress. The planners of a backup and recovery operation must consider whether the EDP facility operates in a way that dependence can be placed on the staff in unusual situations.

Preparations will be different for the handling of personnel dealing with a localized fire or minor disaster as compared to those dealing with a regional disaster, such as extreme weather conditions, floods, hurricanes, tornadoes, etc. It must be constantly remembered that the safety of personnel is of paramount importance, and this will include the safety of their dependents when there is regional danger.

- **Planning Personnel Actions:**

   The planning of personnel actions, moving between sites, possibly crowding into offices and handling unfamiliar tasks, must be carefully considered in detail. People should be informed in advance where they will be expected to report, how they will get there, and what their additional responsibilities will be. In preparation for such moves, it may be necessary to examine floor plans in detail, to have some extra equipment available, to lay in heavier electric power lines, more standby telephone lines, and so on, to be assured that when the people are moved, they will be able to work effectively.

   If two or more sites routinely provide backup to each other during periods of equipment changeover, scheduled maintenance, or minor failure, the personnel will become very familiar with the operation. It will essentially be a continued rehearsal of a disaster situation. In such cases, the people involved should understand the problems of emergency recovery in detail and should be able to make worthwhile suggestions for the plan.

- **Telephone Trees:**

   Part of the preparation for disaster recovery is assembling the names, addresses, and telephone numbers of all persons who may be involved. This is not necessarily as simple as it sounds as many personnel departments do not release the telephone contact information for employees. They consider that home addresses and telephone numbers are confidential information which should not be written down and distributed widely where it could be used for someone else's commercial gain. There is a simple way of circumventing this problem, which must be carefully worked out in advance. Do not publish a single, comprehensive "telephone tree," but merely publish the telephone numbers of the key contacts and their alternates. They, in turn, will have lists of the people they should call, and so on.

Figure 4-5, Disaster Telephone Tree, is a form for organizing a tree by application system or organization group. Of course, a few EDP management people must assemble the complete telephone lists in case there is a breakdown in any part of the chain.

- **Training:**

People must be given sufficient training in the problem being considered, the reason for the plan structure, and their parts in it. This must be training with feedback that is repeated periodically or when there is a change of staff. They must rehearse their roles to the extent necessary and be provided with any skills training that may be required.

Each person must be recognized as an important link in the overall plan. Since most people involved will be quite experienced in their own special areas, they should have their suggestions considered seriously.

One possibility to consider is to offer positive rewards for any outstanding performances during emergencies. This would serve to advise all personnel of the special nature of their activities during and after a security event.

b. **Supplies and Forms Requirements:**

Most supplies are catalog items with reasonable availability. Most facilities have a sufficiently large number and variety of such items to make plans for stockpiling needed supplies at more than one location. Valuable time can be lost, however, if supplies are not carefully cataloged and analyzed. The stores people must be told what will be needed in the event of an emergency.

Paper stocks and forms are obviously the critical area to analyze because many of the forms may be special and very large quantities of some forms may be routinely used. Adequate buffer supplies of stocks should be kept in two or three locations. Vendor information should be available in an emergency for the critical stocks. Many office supplies are available on the open market locally and need not be backed up to any great extent.

61

Updated _____

DISASTER TELEPHONE TREE

Figure 4-5

Application System or Group _____

Key Contact (1)	Extension	Home Phone	Address	Other Personnel To Call (2)	Extension	Home Phone	Position (3)
Alternate (1) Key Contact							

Notes:

1. Each Key Contact will have a more detailed telephone and address list.

2. Normally, the Key Contact on Alternate Key Contact will call the Other Personnel.

3. Note the Key User Contacts first. Some users may not want to be called on weekends. Note this if management approves it.

A strong forms control program can be invaluable in a disaster situation. All forms will be adequately cataloged, with samples, and the information will be available at more than one site. This is most important with specially-printed forms and internally developed forms.

The provision of supplies is not a minor task and must be integrated into the recovery program. Most supplies are stored in basements or near vulnerable areas and, by the nature of paper, they are particularly susceptible to water damage, be it from storm floods or firemen's hoses.

Particular care must be given to the identification and continued availability of critical items in stock and of special forms on which there may be critical dependence. The replacement lead time of such items can be great if adequate backup stocks have not been arranged.

c. **Transportation Requirements:**

There are two transportation problems to be considered in disaster recovery preparation. One is the effect of a regional disaster on public transportation and the ability of employees to get to work and deliveries to be made. The other is the rapid movement of people and supplies to an alternate site and the regular "shuttling" between sites during the security event.

Events which disrupt the transportation of people and supplies over a region cannot be readily overcome and present a serious problem to the ability of the EDP facility to operate effectively. Even overnight accommodations nearby will be difficult to obtain because of the competition for them. Such problems as a wide power failure, earthquakes, labor difficulties, riots, and so on, can generally only be met by locating the backup facility at a considerable distance from the affected facility, and depending upon other personnel to operate it.

If the disaster is localized to the EDP facility, however, and an operating backup site is available within 50 miles, a different set of plans should be prepared. In this case, some personnel will be expected to use their own cars and commute in a different direction. Others will be helped by using public transportation in a different way. Still others, who may normally walk to work or share in ride groups, will need to have shuttle buses arranged from convenient pick-up sites. Plans will have to be made for rapidly renting such buses or vans, getting drivers, and making the schedules known. A number of smaller vehicles may also have to be arranged to move critical personnel and supplies from site to site routinely. Still other arrangements may have to be made to take vans with snacks and drinks to the new site. All such contacts should be made in advance with lists of vendors, telephone numbers, costs, etc., prepared.

d. Facility and Office Space Requirements:

There are two possible objectives in the selection of space into which an EDP facility can be moved after the loss of an original site. They are:

1. Space which can be used temporarily until the original site is restored.

2. Space into which the EDP facility can relocate with relative permanence.

A move from a damaged site to a partially prepared floor space cannot be done rapidly. Cooling water, air conditioners, raised floors, and the like take time to install. It may take several weeks if environmental equipment is to be acquired. Site preparation must be done in advance, if recovery is needed on the same day as the loss of capability or very rapidly. Communications lines, power lines, and ancillary environmental equipment to support the critical functions must be installed well before a problem occurs. Such work is expensive, however, and should not be undertaken unless the need for rapid backup is great or if the site could be used regularly for taking part of the normal data processing load. Plans for space into which the facility can be relocated should therefore reflect, whenever possible, the future growth plans of the organization.

A major consideration in plans for backup space for the computer complex is the ability to provide simultaneous office space for terminal users and other staff on a local basis. Local operations are considerably less complex than remote operations.

e. Power and Environmental Systems Requirements:

Uninterruptible Power Supply (UPS) systems normally fulfill the useful function of protecting against power line transients and other brief interruptions, and thus keep the system running smoothly with fewer restarts and less potential damage to data integrity. They also provide a short period during a primary power failure, during which a standby generator can be brought into operation to support the critical data processing functions. They further provide a useful function in the case of many types of disaster. They provide a short period, usually from fifteen to thirty minutes during which the system can be brought down gracefully without loss of information.

It has been pointed out that power and environmental control systems are the most expensive and time-consuming to bring up at a new site. No reasonable backup can be expected unless the emergency site has been well-prepared in advance with such equipment.

f. Documentation Requirements:

All backup documentation should be analyzed so that needed material is available at the off-site facility in time of need. The best approach for backing up operations documentation and systems programs is to use one of the several word processing or similar library systems available and have all the information in machine-readable form. It can then be routinely backed up with other data and taken to the backup site. There it can be stripped out if needed.

The greatest problem comes from user manuals, system manuals, program manuals, etc. These tend to be given narrow distribution and kept in fire-prone areas such as paper-cluttered offices. One approach is to put them on a library control system and store backup copies at a remote site. However, they then tend not to be updated correctly over time. Another approach is to microfilm all such manuals, at least annually, and store in a secure place. This can be more expensive. The problem of backing up documentation must be studied carefully in the plan preparation phase, even though it is not generally a popular activity.

Of special consideration is the backup of the Disaster Recovery Plan itself. Since it will have details of names, phone numbers, contacts, equipment inventories, alternate site agreements, and so on, that cannot be readily memorized, copies of the Plan must be available immediately at the time a disaster is recognized. This means that copies of the Disaster Recovery Procedures (the Action Plan) must not only be distributed to key locations in the EDP facility and the Information Services offices, but they should also be kept at the homes of the key people who will be contacted in time of emergency.

There are two reasons for keeping copies of the Disaster Recovery Plan at the homes of key individuals. The first is that a serious disaster could keep people from entering the facility and offices. The second is that most physical damage happens at night or on weekends, when it may not be detected in time.

4.5   SELECTION OF RECOVERY STRATEGIES

In the EDP Disaster Recovery Project Plan (Figure 2-2) the alternative recovery strategies are considered after the requirements of the critical resources and applications have been assessed, and a decision has been made on a long-term strategy, or a short-term strategy, or a short-term, high-impact plan. The disaster recovery objectives and the Key Disaster Scenario have also been established.

4.5.1 EVALUATION OF ALTERNATIVE RECOVERY STRATEGIES

A wide range of alternative recovery strategies can be considered. These include:

- Service Degradation Strategies

- Internal Recovery Strategies

- Commercial Recovery Strategies

- Cooperative Recovery Strategies

- Combinations of the Above Strategies

For a small organization, a single strategy will probably be sufficient. For larger organizations, with a variety of users and applications, a principal strategy, with a combination of secondary strategies, is normally the best route. The strategies selected must be based on the functional requirements that have been developed as the Plan has progressed, with any management directives factored in.

A good Disaster Recovery Procedures Manual has a great many specific details in it so that some decisions are already made. The recovery strategies are the key to these details. Therefore, the evaluation and selection of the recovery strategies is the key to optimizing the design and development phase of preparing the Plan. The evaluation and selection of the strategies should include:

- Requirements based on priorities

- Consideration of a variety of possible strategies

- Cost analysis of alternative strategies

- Selection of acceptable strategies based on the requirements.

Figure 4-6, Acceptable Recovery Strategies for Applications, is a worksheet that can be used to list the application systems in priority order, with the maximum acceptable recovery time for each, as determined by management. The most probable strategy, or strategies, for each system can then be entered. Cost estimates should then be made for the development and preparation of the strategies, at least for the critical systems, and the daily cost of the strategy in use. These costs need only be rough estimates at first. They will be refined as the critical application systems and their recovery strategies are further defined.

Figure 4-7, Matrix of Recovery Possibilities, lists a number of the alternative recovery strategies which will be discussed below. It roughly indicates the types of strategies that are reasonable, depending on the maximum acceptable recovery times for the application systems.

These two figures are key to an analysis of alternative recovery strategies. The application systems must be fitted to recovery strategies with acceptable costs and recovery times.

Figure 4-6

ACCEPTABLE RECOVERY STRATEGIES FOR APPLICATIONS

Application System	Priority	Maximum Acceptable Recovery Time	Most Probable Acceptable Recovery Strategy	Estimated Cost	
				Preparation	In Use (Daily)
Critical					
Non-Critical					

Figure 4-7

MATRIX OF RECOVERY POSSIBILITIES

Maximum Acceptable Recovery Time	Alternative Recovery Strategies										
	Internal			Commercial					Cooperative		
	Degrade Service	Second Site	Available Space	Service Bureaus	Equipped ROC	Shell ROC	Time Brokers	Hardware Vendors	Mutual Aid	Equipped ROC	Shell ROC
1 Hour		x									
8 Hours		x		x				x	x		
24 Hours		x		x	x		x	x	x	x	
7 Days		x	x	x	x	x	x	x	x	x	x
14 Days or More	x	x	x	x	x	x	x	x	x	x	x

4.5.2   SERVICE DEGRADATION STRATEGIES

Only a few organizations who have an EDP facility will not be seriously harmed if they are forced to do without it for more than two weeks. There are some, organizations, however, and there are many users in all organizations, who can do without their application systems for some time. When dependence on EDP is not immediate and critical, it is usually assumed that the original hardware and services can be repaired or replaced in time to avoid major loss. Other dependencies, such as people, data, and programs, must be suitably protected through the outage period. It is important to note, however, that the initial belief that backup of hardware facilities is not required does not provide justification for ignoring contingency planning. There may be a number of dependencies that are not immediately obvious. Further, a sound risk analysis should support any conclusion that backup arrangements are not required. There are three types of service degradation strategies that are usually considered:

- Reduction of Service Response

- Manual Procedures

- Withdrawal of Services

a.   Reduction of Service Response:

This strategy rarely applies to transaction-oriented, communications-dependent facilities, although in many cases, a backup operation will not give as rapid response as the original system. This strategy is normally considered for lower-priority batch applications which can be picked up and transported to other locations, and run when feasible. It is essentially a strategy of running lower priority jobs without firm schedules, and with little priority.

b.   Manual Procedures:

For a number of application systems, and sometimes for whole EDP facilities, reversion to manual procedures is still a possibility, and should be seriously considered for a disaster situation. Typical systems that can revert to manual procedures are analytical programs that can be handled on hand calculators or minicomputers. There is always a danger to the future EDP effort when this happens, as some analysts and engineers prefer such an approach in any event. Another class of systems that may revert to manual on occasion are point-of-sale terminals in smaller stores, and production control systems on machine-shop floors. The organization may well want to keep in operation in a crippled state by reverting to manual methods, instead of losing hours or days of operation.

c.   Withdrawal of Services:

There are some application systems, such as long-range analytical and planning work, and some classes of developmental work, where the obvious strategy may be to simply not perform the calculations until the computer center has recovered from the disaster. Many corporate analyses must be on the computer, as they have become too complex to do by hand, yet have long time horizons. Such calculations frequently require that many different data files be mounted in order to run, and would be almost impossible to operate under emergency conditions.

4.5.3   INTERNAL RECOVERY STRATEGIES

The most effective and efficient EDP disaster recovery strategy is to have internal organizational control over all the backup facilities and systems to be used in an emergency.

- The hardware systems can be maintained at the best configuration.

- Test runs can be made at the convenience of the organization.

- Security controls can be placed equally on all facilities.

- The systems can be made available whenever management requires.

Such internal backup facilities can be of two general types: equipped facilities or empty shells. These will be discussed, as well as criteria for site selection.

a.   Multiple EDP Facilities:

Multiple EDP facilities in a single organization can be achieved by dividing the required EDP facilities into at least two geographically separate locations. The smallest location must be able to carry the critical work load for the time needed to reestablish the inoperative facility. This strategy does not necessarily imply the installation of excess capacity great enough to carry the critical work. It only implies the physical dispersion of the normal capability into two or more locations. Each location could be doing useful work ordinarily. On the other hand, if the computer operations are sufficiently important or sensitive, such as on-line operation of the business, an organization may decide to have full backup internally without being concerned about the excess capacity represented.

The economic feasibility of this strategy for most organizations is based on the assumption that, for the majority of facilities, the critical work load is less than 50%, and may be less than 20%, of the total load. Thus, no increase in total EDP capacity may be required above that normally installed. Hardware often does not divide cleanly into two halves to handle the required systems, but there is usually no requirement to have precisely 50% at each site. Any split which will suit the need for processing the critical work at either location is adequate, provided that the backup facility can reduce its work load in an emergency to include only its critical functions.

70

To realize all the potential benefits of the multiple-internal-location option, it is necessary that full capacity to run all the critical work load is installed at both locations. This generally implies the availability of the full range of all essential resources to be available at both sites. This can mean significant added costs but may be necessary for the organization. Companies which depend on their computer systems for their basic operations will probably want to install full, dual backup systems. Others may be content with smaller backup systems.

b. Available Rooms or "Empty Shells:"

Available rooms for backup purposes are sometimes called "empty shells." They are spaces sufficiently large, and environmentally controllable, to install a replacement computer that has been rapidly obtained after a disaster event. They can be of two types: completely bare or a "ready room."

A "ready room" is a facility in a building with sufficient power and communications lines, a raised floor, air conditioning and environmental controls, and physical controls, but no data processing hardware. A "bare room" is simply a building with available floor space. There have been no preparations made. Such preparations are normally quite time-consuming.

The empty shell thus provides a planned site to rapidly install replacement hardware when it is needed. A successful recovery in such a contingency center environment requires that there be:

- An adequate probability that all the vendors of critically needed units can deliver soon enough to restore operations before unacceptable losses occur. This implies at least several days before operation is restored, at the best.

- An adequate plan to return from the shell to the permanent site with an acceptable level of disruption.

- A shell site that is sufficiently close to the permanent site to avoid severe problems with personnel availability.

The best use of the empty shell for disaster backup is, normally, for the second backup site to handle the bulk of the application systems after the critical systems have been handled rapidly at a prime site.

c. Site Selection Criteria:

When a site is to be selected and prepared for disaster recovery backup, considerable thought should go into its selection to get the best returns on the money spent. There are a number of criteria which should be considered in the selection process:

- Is the site suitable in the future for the normal expansion of the EDP function?

- Could the site be used for normal operations?

- Can employees get there conveniently? Are there good roads, protected parking facilities, and bus service?

- Is it in a good area for telephone and messenger service communications?

- Are there reasonable lunch room or fast-food facilities within walking distance, or could an in-house lunch room or a truck canteen service be used?

- Is the area considered safe for night-shift workers?

The Disaster Recovery Planning Team should go to some effort on site selection. Frequently, the first ideas that are put forward are found to have flaws. All considered sites should be visited, and their merits discussed with the Engineering or Buildings Department personnel. **Figure 4-8, Internal Backup Site Checklist,** will aid in this on-site inspection and analysis.

4.5.4   COMMERCIAL RECOVERY STRATEGIES

Because of the widespread need for disaster recovery backup services, a great many commercial offerings are available. Some are widely advertised in the literature. Some are listed in the FTP Technical Library publication, "EDP Security Manual." Many will provide detailed literature describing their services. The variety includes:

- Commercial Service Bureaus

- Equipped Recovery Operation Centers (ROC)

- Ready Rooms or Empty Shell ROC's

- Time Brokers

- Hardware Vendor Facilities

a.   Commercial Service Bureaus:

Commercial service bureaus offer both batch services with pickup and delivery, and on-line, or timesharing services. If the service bureau is large enough to handle the work being considered for disaster recovery, it will expect to make sales presentations, hold

Figure 4-8

INTERNAL BACKUP SITE CHECKLIST

Site _____   Date _____

1. **Vicinity:**
   - Nearby Buildings   --
   - Employee Parking   --
   - Nearby Food and Motel   --

2. **Premises:**
   - Facilities and Maintenance   --
   - Signs and Access Control   --
   - Power and Telephone Lines   --
   - Other Company Operations   --

3. **Computer Room:**
   - Access Control   --
   - Air Conditioning   --
   - Environmental Control   --
   - Electric Panels   --
   - Telephone Panels   --
   - Hazards   --

4. **Tape Library:**
   - Access Control   --
   - Sufficient Space   --
   - Housekeeping Problems   --

5. **Terminals:**
   - Facilities   --
   - Space for Desks and CRT's   --
   - Control   --

6. **Data Preparation:**
   - Staff Space   --
   - Facilities   --
   - Equipment Space   --

7. **Other Equipment:**
   - Electrical   --
   - Environmental   --
   - Burster/Decollector/Mailing   --
   - File   --
   - Other   --

8. **Administrative:**
   - Fire Hazards   --
   - Fire Equipment   --
   - Waste Disposal   --
   - Dock Control   --

9. **User Groups:**
   - Desk Space   --
   - Source Data Handling   --

discussions, and have a contract signed. Most service bureaus will not contractually obligate themselves to hold reserved time on their computer waiting for your disaster. They must, therefore, be large enough to readily absorb the extra load in an emergency. If an agreement for future possible services is signed with a service bureau, the normal steps taken are then:

- You are established as a customer by signing a contract and are given access information and codes.

- Your people attend classes in their particular systems and languages.

- You convert the Job Control Language statements of your critical systems to fit their operating system.

- You use existing object decks and run tests to determine compatibility.

- You store all required source decks, object decks, and data onto one of their disks and begin payment for it.

- You try some test runs by simulating a disaster event.

Since this is the service bureau's business, it can normally be handled smoothly. It is usually fairly costly to maintain, however. There are frequently up-front costs and minimum charges. There are also the charges for the ongoing storage of your material on the disks, and for the various tests which should be run.

The service bureau approach is particularly good for such critical systems as payroll, which must be run at specified times, disaster or not. One problem with service bureaus, as with other commercial services, is that there may be configuration or JCL changes from time to time which cause extra effort and cost.

b. **Equipped Recovery Operation Centers (ROC):**

Equipped contingency centers, or the computer-in-place concept, have been widely advertised and discussed, but only a few are available. These are complete EDP facilities, and include communications capabilities and office space for your employees. Some operate as service bureaus, but discontinue the provision of some services when a subscriber has a need for a portion of the backup center. Others are used only to rehearse contingency plans and to assure the operation of critical functions on the backup equipment during an emergency.

The planned use of an equipped ROC requires the prior consideration of several factors, such as:

- Compatibility of hardware.

- Restoration of communications. This can be a complex problem if the main node of a network must be changed.

- The cost of initial occupancy. The cost of "declaring an emergency" may be great, in which case you may have second thoughts about using the service during a minor security event when the service could be very helpful.

- The security problem if other organizations are sharing the same facility.

- Availability of the facility for rehearsal.

- Possibility of too many subscribers needing the facility at the same time.

- Distance for key people to travel from the permanent site. Subsequent recovery at the home site could be difficult if the key staff are too far removed.

The more successful of the equipped ROCs have strong telecommunications facilities installed, and have made network surveys and backup network designs with their clients. Their services may include:

- Backup Network Design

- Backup Network Optimization

- Communications Facilities Procurement

- Backup Network Installation

- Network Diagnostics and Maintenance

Because of the complexity of such operations, the subscription fees are normally high. Some typical fees are:

Service	Fee
Regular Monthly Standby Fee:	From $2,000 to $8,000
Disaster Usage Daily Fee:	From $4,000 to $10,000
Ready Space Occupancy Fee:	From $400 to $800 (per day)
Disaster Initiation Fee:	From $20,000 to $60,000 (depending on speed of access)
Network Design and Installation:	Varies up to $25,000
Communications Costs:	Varied

The ROCs offer an excellent service. In addition to the cost, there are some disadvantages for most users, however:

1. They restrict the direction and expansion of individual members to maintain minimum acceptable compatibility with the backup site.

2. Recovery procedures will require regular maintenance because of configuration changes demanded by the overall needs of the group.

3. They are generally based on the assumption that only two or three subscribers out of 30 or more will have simultaneous disasters.

c. Ready Rooms or Empty Shell (ROCs):

Several companies have constructed large, empty computer facilities at selected locations across the country. They provide these "Empty Shells" as alternate computer rooms for companies which enter into a contract with them. In the event of a disaster, the client company is provided use of these ready rooms to assemble a backup computer system.

These facilities are arranged the same as the available rooms or empty shells described under "Internal Recovery Strategies." They have the same advantages and problems. They are cheaper than equipped rooms, but slower to start up. In commercial ready rooms, there should be reasonable arrangements made for limiting the number of organizations which might simultaneously need the shell. They should not be chosen because of their economy without realizing that it will probably take four to seven days, as a minimum, to have the needed equipment delivered, installed, tested, and made to work with your required operating system.

However, they offer a very good alternative for secondary backup of the less critical application systems.

d. Time Brokers:

In this strategy, a third party, or broker, finds another site that a company can use in the event of a disaster. The broker guarantees the availability of predetermined computer facilities to be used as it is agreed the work can fit in. All decisions on the facility and the contractual terms are made with the broker. A typical agreement is shown in **Figure 4-9, Computer Service Backup Agreement.**

Normally, a broker arranges with several companies in a geographical area to reserve excess computer time on their computers to be used by other companies when needed. The broker charges a set monthly fee. The user also pays the site owner for the computer resources used.

Figure 4-9
(Page 1)

TYPICAL AGREEMENT WITH TIME BROKER

COMPUTER SERVICE BACKUP AGREEMENT

Agreement entered into this _____ day of _____, 19___ by and between <u>Computer Service Company</u> and _____ having an office for the transaction of business at_____

_____

_____

hereinafter referred to as the Customer.

WITNESSETH

Whereas, the Customer desires to have available for its use certain back-up data processing capabilities and services compatible with its present facility operations which consist of:

Whereas,_____represents that it has compatible back-up data processing equipment available for Customer's use during designated times,

NOW, THEREFORE, IN CONSIDERATION OF THE MUTUAL COVENANTS AND PROMISES CONTAINED HEREIN, IT IS AGREED AS FOLLOWS:

1. _____hereby designates _____ having an office for the transaction of business at _____

   _____
   as the back-up installation at which there is data processing equipment compatible to Customer's data processing equipment above described, and which will be available for use by the Customer in accordance with the terms and conditions herein.

2. The data processing facilities and equipment shall be available to the Customer during the following times:

   Days _____ from _____ to _____

   Days _____ from _____ to _____

   and for a maximum of _____ hours per week.

Figure 4-9
(Page 2)

TYPICAL AGREEMENT WITH TIME BROKER

COMPUTER SERVICE BACKUP AGREEMENT

3. The data processing equipment will be available for Customer's use at the designated times for a maximum of_____ continuous weeks. After such continuous use period, the facilities will not be available for subsequent use until seven calendar days thereafter.

4. Customer agrees to pay _____ a service charge of $_____ per month payable in advance and an hourly rate of $_____ for all use of the equipment at the designated installation. Charges for hourly use of the equipment at the installation shall be paid to _____ within thirty days of invoice.

5. If a designated installation is not available by reason of equipment malfunction, power failure or any other causes beyond the control of _____ , including, without limitation, acts of God, acts of public administators, decrees, war, riots, labor disturbances, strikes, civil commotion, and the like, _____ _____ shall use its best efforts to locate an alternative installation compatible with Customer's equipment. If the equipment at such alternate installation is of more advanced design and, therefore, capable of completing Customer's output in less time than the equipment at the designated installation, the charges for use of such alternate installation shall be based upon the normal hourly operating time of the equipment at the designated installation, if such equipment were used to produce the equivalent output.

6. Unless unavailable by reason of an occurrence set forth in Paragraph 5 herein, the data processing facilities at the designated installation shall be available for a minimum of _____ hours per week and for _____ weeks per month at the base hourly rate set forth herein, and if additional time is requested and is available, the hourly rate for such time shall be $_____.

7. _____ represents that the equipment at the above designated installation is basically compatible with the Customer's equipment above set forth, however, Customer shall test the equipment at the designated installation for compatibility purposes once each calendar quarter to assure continued compatibility. Charges for the use of the equipment during such test periods will be at the normal hourly rate set forth herein, and such test shall be for a period of 2 hours.

8. Customer agrees to provide all operating personnel and software support at the designated installation and shall notify _____ of its intention to make use of the data processing equipment 4 hours prior to making any use of the facilities at the designated installation.

Figure 4-9
(Page 3)

TYPICAL AGREEMENT WITH TIME BROKER

COMPUTER SERVICE BACKUP AGREEMENT

9. _____ agrees to provide, at the designated installation, security services and reasonable work area and space for Customer's use during such time as the installation is in use by the Customer. Storage space for use by the Customer will be provided if same is available.

10. Within three hours of request by Customer, _____ shall provide transportation services to pick up cards, tapes, disk packs, and other material required for the operation of Customer's program at the installation and shall thereafter deliver same to the installation.

11. _____ shall have the right to change designated installations on thirty days notice to Customer; however, if such change is effected within a calendar quarter in which a compatibility test has been conducted by Customer at the prior installation, a test of equal duration at the new installation will be made available without hourly charge to the Customer.

12. The services under this agreement shall be first available on _____, and the agreement shall continue for a period of one year thereafter; however, either party may cancel the agreement on thirty days written notice to the other by Certified Mail, Return Receipt Requested, at the respective addresses above designated.

13. Upon termination of this agreement, the Customer shall remove all of its materials which may be stored at the installation within fifteen days, and upon failure to do so, _____ may remove and dispose of same at the expense of Customer.

14. It is agreed that in the event that material and data received by _____ for transportation to the installation and/or used at the installation are lost or destroyed through equipment failure, or act of _____, the sole liability, if any, shall be limited to the cost required to regenerate the lost data from Customer's supporting materials on such equipment deemed suitable by _____ for such regeneration. If the Customer has not maintained such supporting material, the liability of _____, if any, shall be limited to cost of such regeneration had the supporting material been available. The supporting material for the purpose of this agreement is defined as exact copies of the punch cards, magnetic tapes, disks, or other data, excluding records and data not in machine-readable form.

15. In no event shall the liability of _____ arising out of the furnishing of devices hereunder, or the use of the installation, exceed the price paid in service charges for the month in which the error from which the liability results occurred.

Figure 4-9
(Page 4)

TYPICAL AGREEMENT WITH TIME BROKER

COMPUTER SERVICE BACKUP AGREEMENT

16. _____ shall have no liability for general, special, or consequential damages, or for any loss, damages, or expenses directly or indirectly arising from the services or installation time furnished hereunder, or for any inability to use them, or for any other cause including, but not limited to, failure beyond its control.

17. The Customer agrees that it shall not, for a period of one year from the date hereof, attempt to purchase or lease computer time, equipment, or services directly from any backup installation assigned by _____ pursuant to this agreement.

In Witness Whereof, the parties hereto have hereunto set their hands the day and year first above written.

_____

By _____

Customer _____

By _____

This is a fairly reasonable approach, and can work if good relationships develop between the companies involved. There is normally a list of possibilities, and a convenient site can be arranged. However, there are serious problems with maintaining system compatibility over time, and with being assured of availability when there is an emergency.

Normally, the computer time broker has all interested companies fill out an initial, simple questionnaire, similar to **Figure 4-10, Configuration Questionnaire,** to make an initial screening of possible compatibility and to discuss the possibilities with prospective clients.

e. Hardware Vendor Facilities:

Seldom do hardware vendors or large systems have demonstration or service bureau computers that are available to users in times of disaster, but there are some exceptions, and they should be investigated. Normally, the systems that are run by hardware vendors have constantly-changing configurations, or special features, that make reasonable compatibility difficult. In addition, hardware vendor facilities are usually showcases, and have difficult security problems.

Hardware vendors of medium to small computers are an excellent source of backup equipment, however. In the lower ranges, computers tend to be much more standardized, with fewer operating system variations.

Hardware vendor facilities are particularly good backup sites for key entry computers, certain office automation applications, engineering computers, and the like. Vendors are also generally eager to make reasonable arrangements with their users, and will work day and night to help them restore their computer operation in an emergency. Hardware vendors have been known to turn display offices into secure facilities to aid a client in an emergency.

4.5.5   COOPERATIVE RECOVERY STRATEGIES

A number of companies near various large cities have pooled their planning resources to save everyone money. Some have formed legal associations for the protection of all parties. Formal contracts or simple reciprocal agreements are exchanged. The details depend on the type of industry or whether trade secrets may be involved.

a.   Reciprocal Agreements:

Reciprocal, or mutual aid, agreements are conceptually possible when one facility can accept the work of another temporarily inoperative facility. Technically, the transportability of work between two facilities requires that data and programs from one be acceptable to

Figure 4-10

CONFIGURATION QUESTIONNAIRE
(Example)

Company Name _____

Address _____

City/State _____ Zip _____

Phone (Day) _____ Contact _____

Phone (Night) _____ Contact _____

Computer _____ Core Size _____

Operating System _____ Release _____

Tapes		Disks	Spindles		
1600/6250	____	3330 ____	____	Card Readers	____
1600	____	3340 ____	____	Read Punches	____
D/D	____	3350 ____	____	Printers	____
800	____	Other ____	____	L.P.M.	____
Other	____				

Other Peripheral Equipment _____

System Assignments

Tapes	____	To	____	Readers	____
Disks	____	To	____	Punches	____
Typewriter	_____			Other	____
Printers	_____	Trains	____	_____	

* Shift Rates

	Shift Hours	Rates	Available Hours
1st	_____	_____	_____
2nd	_____	_____	_____
3rd	_____	_____	_____

Discounts _____

Machine Features _____

Packages _____

Accommodations _____

* If your rates are based on a per unit utilization, attach rate schedule.

the other with only modest changes. Rehearsals are most helpful, but they are usually costly and generate unwelcome disruptions in the "backup" organization. The rehearsals should include full operation of the critical functions. These practice sessions should be thoroughly realistic and not dependent on the use of any resources from the inoperative facility. Such rehearsals are difficult to conduct in a mutual aid environment, since compatibility of the backup system can only be assured if the critical functions are run realistically at the backup facility as part of the normal job stream, with test data, files, etc. This can, of course, be done off-shift, if necessary.

It is difficult to make mutual aid agreements totally reliable. Changes in either system may render the arrangement invalid. Further, management shifts may invalidate the arrangements without prior notice, leaving a previously supported facility without backup.

While mutual aid agreements are conceptually feasible, they rarely prove workable when needed except for medium and smaller systems. The high risk of discovering in time of need that the backup is not actually available is generally too great to warrant confidence in this strategy for larger computer operations.

Reciprocal agreements can be either formal or informal, and either bilateral or with a group. **Figure 4-11, Contingency Backup Arrangement for Toally Disabled Computer Equipment,** is a sample of an informal reciprocal agreement. When the agreement is to be informal and bilateral, it is usually common to simply exchange "letters of understanding" between the organizations, signed by a manager who can stand behind the agreement. These agreements are not legally binding. **Figure 4-12, Sample Letter of Understanding,** is an example of such an agreement. Such letters, of course, need to be reaffirmed when managers change. The Security Coordinator should keep up-to-date on such agreements.

Some industries, such as banking, frequently have many users on similar vendor equipment and running similar programs. In these industries, there is, when needed, helpful exchange of backup capability in an emergency for the good of the public and the image of the industry. For example, when a bank in Hartford, Connecticut, had its power lines accidentally broken by a contractor in 1980, it soon had all its key programs running at a number of different banks.

b. Cooperative Recovery Operation Centers (ROCs):

In several large cities, the computer-in-place concept has been handled cooperatively. One such organization is LSCUBA (Large Scale Computer Users Backup Association), which was formed in the Philadelphia area in 1977 by 14 varied users. It was formed to study and provide a viable solution to the problem of computer disaster recovery and to contract for a group backup center. It received a number of facilities management bids to run the projected facility. It proved to be competitive; and by the end of 1977, 27 companies had signed up.

Figure 4-11
(Page 1)

CONTINGENCY BACKUP ARRANGEMENT
FOR TOTALLY-DISABLED COMPUTER EQUIPMENT

(Sample provided by Greater Boston Computer Backup Group)

Purpose: Each of the undersigned parties (each of whom is herein called a "Company" and collectively the "Companies") hereby recognizes and acknowledges (i) the possibility of a total disabling of its batch processing computer equipment (herein called its "Equipment") and (ii) its desire to safeguard itself from the consequences of such an occurrence to the extent possible by means of the informal, non-legal Contingency Backup Arrangement evidenced hereby.

Contingency Backup Arrangement: In the event that a total disabling of any Company's Equipment shall occur, the Company whose Equipment has been totally disabled (such Company being herein called the "User") shall inform each of the other Companies of such occurrence (each such other Company being herein called a "Provider" and collectively the "Providers"). In the event that a majority of the Providers shall concur in the User's determination that the User's Equipment is totally disabled, then the User shall become entitled to utilize such of the Equipment of the respective Providers as is specified in the respective Providers' Exhibits (any Equipment specified in any Provider's Exhibit being herein called such Provider's "Offered Equipment").

Any utilization by any User of any Provider's Offered Equipment shall be subject to the terms and conditions set forth in the respective Provider's Exhibit.

Notwithstanding anything to the contrary appearing herein or in any Exhibit, however, each Provider's obligation to allow any User to utilize said Provider's Offered Equipment during the hours and days specified in said Provider's Exhibit shall terminate 60 days after the total disabling of said User's Equipment. If at any time subsequent to said total disabling, however, said User renders its Equipment (whether by repair or replacement) operable to an extent sufficient to enable said Company to serve as a Provider should the occasion arise, then each Provider shall again become obligated to provide said Company with said Provider's Offered Equipment in the event that said Company suffers another total disabling of its Equipment (although each Provider's obligation to do so shall again terminate 60 days after said subsequent total disabling).

Provider's Exhibits: Each Company shall set forth, in a separate Exhibit attached hereto, the following information: (i) the Offered Equipment which it shall make available to any User (specifying the various types and amounts of such Offered Equipment, which Offered Equipment shall constitute a dedicated system owned or leased by the respective Provider); (ii) the approximate geographic location of said Offered Equipment (which Offered Equipment shall be located in an installation owned or leased by the respective Provider); and (iii) the days of the week on which and the hours of such days during which any User may utilize said Offered Equipment.

Figure 4-11
(Page 2)

CONTINGENCY BACKUP ARRANGEMENT
FOR TOTALLY-DISABLED COMPUTER EQUIPMENT

Multiple Users: In the event that there are two or more Companies which qualify as Users during the same period of time and said Users desire to utilize the Offered Equipment on a pro rata basis (without in any way limiting said Users' respective rights to utilize the Offered Equipment of each of the other Providers). Moreover, the fact that a Provider has made its Offered Equipment available to one or more Users shall in no way affect its obligation to make its Offered Equipment available to any other Users (regardless of whether or not any other Provider has previously done so).

Security Precautions and Liability Provisions: Any User who utilizes the Offered Equipment of any Provider shall adhere to whatever security arrangements are put into effect by said Provider with respect to said User's utilization of such Offered Equipment.

Each User shall reimburse the Provider for any repair or replacement costs incurred by the Provider as a result of any physical damage to or disabling of the respective Offered Equipment caused by such User's negligent utilization thereof. No User shall be liable for any damage or disablement attributable to normal wear and tear, however.

Utilization Costs: In the event of an emergency situation arising which causes the provisions of this agreement to be put into effect, charges for the use of computer equipment may be made if specified in the Provider's exhibit, or if agreed previously between individual user and provider companies. For testing purposes, however, no reimbursement will be made for the use of equipment, except as provided for elsewhere in this agreement.

No provider shall be obligated to provide any personnel (whether technical, security, or otherwise), programs, or other such additional resources, except insofar as is necessary to render its Offered Equipment readily available to and operable by the User. To the extent that any Provider does provide any such personnel or additional such resources, said Provider shall be reimbursed by the appropriate User for the costs of providing such personnel and additional resources.

Withdrawals: In the event that any Company decides to withdraw from the contingency backup arrangement evidenced hereby, said Company shall notify each of the other Companies of said decision in writing, in which event said Company shall be deemed to have withdrawn from the above-specified arrangement 60 days after written notification is transmitted to the other Companies.

Figure 4-11
(Page 3)

CONTINGENCY BACKUP ARRANGEMENT
FOR TOTALLY-DISABLED COMPUTER EQUIPMENT

Amendments and Modifications: In the event that any Company desires to amend or otherwise modify this instrument or the above-specified arrangement evidenced hereby, no such amendment or modification shall become effective until transmitted in writing to (and accepted in writing by) each of the other Companies.

Non-Legal Nature of Arrangement: Notwithstanding anything to the contrary appearing herein, it is expressly understood and agreed by each of the parties hereto that <u>this instrument and the contingency backup arrangement evidenced hereby are informal and non-legal in nature and wholly unenforceable at law or in equity.</u> This instrument simply evidences an informal, good faith understanding and arrangement which is wholly non-contractual and not binding in any way on any party hereto, none of which parties shall incur any legally enforceable obligation or liability as a result of its execution and delivery hereof and not withstanding its or any other Company's subsequent reliance upon or adherence to either this instrument or the contingency backup arrangement evidenced hereby.

Now, therefore, the undersigned parties have caused this instrument to be executed (without, as specified above, any legal effect whatsoever) by their respective officers, as of December 31, 1975.

Revised: January, 1976

Figure 4-12

SAMPLE LETTER OF UNDERSTANDING

Date _____

Name_____

_____

_____

Dear _____:

    Thank you for the helpful meeting regarding mutual emergency backup for handling computer work in the event of a disastrous occurrence in either of our computer centers. The following is my understanding of the informal reciprocal agreement which was decided would be feasible.

    In the event of a disaster affecting, or a major breakdown of, either computer system, the other center agrees to aid in the recovery and production of high priority work on the affected systems to the best of its ability and consistent with its own work load and the time.

    The affected center would take its input forms and source data, and any magnetic media available, to the other center at a mutually agreed time. This would probably be weekday evening shifts. The host center would make the necessary arrangements with its security guards and would offer some technical support on the first session to be sure the systems were brought up correctly and were operating as expected.

    This mutual emergency backup assistance would probably only be required for a few days since the affected center would be actively attempting to get deliveries of replacement equipment from the vendors to be set up in their own offices. We have been assured by _____ that the highest priority would be put on such replacement deliveries in the event of a disaster.

    To prepare for the remote possibility of the need for mutual backup assistance, it was agreed that informal tests would be made of the compatibilities of the systems at a convenient time to both parties.

    Neither _____ nor _____ would charge the other for such help as it would only be requested in emergency situations on an informal basis.

                            Sincerely,

This type of cooperative backup association is based upon having sufficient computer power standing by to service the largest participating member. That computer power can be used as an EDP service bureau on an interruptible basis when not required for disaster backup, or for the great deal of systems development and testing that is needed for creating and maintaining the members' backup systems. It also requires that the criteria for a "disaster" are mutually agreed upon. It assumes that there may be problems if more than two participants have a disaster situation simultaneously.

c. **Cooperative Ready Rooms or Empty Shell ROCs:**

Some organizations have discussed the idea of cooperative contingency centers, called ready rooms, or empty shells. There is less advantage in savings in this concept, because the reduced costs from a fully equipped ROC are offset by the added inconvenience of geographic distance in any cooperative venture. Its low cost, however, means it will continue to be considered.

Cooperative ready rooms have similar advantages and disadvantages to in-house or commercial ready rooms. One of the main advantages is that the special, controlled structure and the environmental control equipment is obtained in advance of any problem. It is always more time-consuming to put together than is the hardware configuration that goes into it.

4.5.6 SELECTION OF COMBINATION STRATEGIES

Very few organizations need full, rapid backup of their total application systems portfolio. Most organizations have a critical group of application systems which must be backed up rapidly, a larger group of systems that must be backed up in reasonable time, from two days to two weeks, and a number of systems that do not need backup for one or two months.

These systems do not all need to be handled by the same strategies. The EDP Disaster Recovery Team should discuss the list of applications and their requirements generated in Figure 4-6, Acceptable Recovery Strategies for Applications, and group different priorities of applications in different strategies that are cost-effective for each group's needs. For example, for an organization:

- Some accounting programs may be backed up within hours on a computer-in-place.

- Certain operational programs may be backed up in batch operation at a service bureau the next day.

- A number of engineering programs may be backed up with a time-sharing service.

- Some data input and check handling programs may be backed up at a cooperating center on the next evening shift.

- A few analytical programs may not be backed up until extra computer equipment is brought into the ready room and tested, possibly taking several weeks.

It will be the job of the Disaster Recovery Team to pull together a combination of strategies, application by application, analyzing the requirements of each. **Figure 4-13, Combination of Disaster Recovery Strategies,** is a visual presentation of this problem.

4.6   COST ANALYSIS FOR DISASTER RECOVERY PLANNING

In a study of EDP security and disaster recovery, a number of good plans and desirable measures will likely be proposed. An analysis should be made to compare the cost of the measures with the possible costs of disruption to the organization.

First, the possible security events must be considered and analyzed as to their probability of occurrence. Second, each specific disaster recovery strategy designed to meet these incidents should be studied independently, considering its priority level and need. These disaster costs, and the recovery strategies to reduce them, may be presented for comparison in either tabular form, as shown, or simply as a memo description. All assumptions of probability of occurrence should be stated. Senior management must decide their preference, and the order of priorities, based on the recommendations of the study team. Forms are attached to aid in performing this series of summary steps.

This section is a simple approach to cost analysis, which will probably be needed at least for budget purposes. If more detailed calculations are required, it may be necessary to perform a risk analysis, as noted in Section 4.7, Risk Analysis. Some organizations will want this full analysis, but they are in the minority. Most organizations will be satisfied with the understanding that:

- there is a definite possibility of a disaster occurring;

- there are legal and operational requirements to protect against great disruption of the EDP operations;

- there are a number of alternative strategies available; so

- which are the best and most-effective strategies?

4.6.1   COST OF POSSIBLE LOSSES

In discussing the probability of disruptions and the probable costs with user management, a serious problem will normally arise. The probable costs given by different users will not be directly comparable, since they will be based on different assumptions. Some users will plead importance, but will have no wish to pay for security. Other users will underestimate the catastrophe to their operations in the event of a major data processing breakdown. Still other users will ask for high reliability, and will back up their requests with sufficient available funds.

Figure 4-13

COMBINATION OF DISASTER RECOVERY STRATEGIES

EDP DISASTER RECOVERY APPROACHES

Application System	Priority Group
A	1
B	1
C	1
D	2
E	2
F	3
G	3
H	3
I	3
J	4
K	4
L	5
M	5
N	6
O	6

Strategy 1
Strategy 2
Strategy 3
Strategy 4
Strategy 5
Strategy 6

Time

The data processing manager must, therefore, resort to an analytical statement of the problems. He should list the probability of occurrence of disruption as it is given, the probable costs, and the costs of security solutions as he perceives them. To help prepare this analysis systematically, and to aid in visualizing the problem, three worksheets are given.

Figure 4-14: Probability of Occurrence of Security Event

This worksheet helps state the most likely problem areas in a form that can be used either judgmentally or as part of calculations. Assumptions are crystallized.

Figure 4-15: Probable Economic Loss

This worksheet gives an analysis of types of loss under varying considerations.

The **Probability of Occurrence Worksheet (Figure 4-14)** is intended to define, by type of asset, the probability of occurrence of security events for each of several threats. Determination of the potential cost of disasters for each of the categories of assets is the objective of the **Probable Economic Loss form (Worksheet 4-15).**

The objective of these two worksheets is to facilitate determination of the areas of greatest exposure. In areas where probability of occurrence and economic loss combine to produce great potential business exposure, prime consideration must be given.

Figure 4-16: Possible Costs of Disaster Recovery Strategies

This worksheet gives a summary of the possible costs of measures for each disaster recovery strategy considered. It does not aid in developing the detail making up the costs. These costs can be balanced against the economic losses, by groups of applications and related recovery strategies, considering the probability of the occurrence of the losses.

Figure 4-14

PROBABILITY OF OCCURRENCE OF SECURITY EVENT

	Fire	Flood	DESTRUCTION Earthquake	Accident	Sabotage	Other	Fraud Theft, Etc.	Employee Error
EDP Equipment								
Installation Facilities								
Data								
Programs Operating System								
Documentation								

Probability of Occurrence Codes: (Enter in Boxes)

1. High Probability

2. Medium Probability

3. Low Probability

Assumptions made for Probability of Occurrence:

Figure 4-15

PROBABLE ECONOMIC LOSS
(Dollars in Thousands)

	Replacement or Reconstruction Cost		Performance Failure Loss									
	Without Backup	With Backup	Without Backup			Current Backup			Desired Backup		
			ETR	EE	BIL	ETR	EE	BIL	ETR	EE	BIL
EDP Equipment											
Installation Facility											
Data											
Programs Operating System											
Documentation											
Total											

Note: ETR: Estimated Time to Recover (Days)   EE: Extra Expense ($000)   BIL: Business Interruption Loss ($000)

Desired Backup (In this space identify the Desired Backup capability with one-time cost plus annual continuing cost.

Figure 4-16

POSSIBLE COSTS OF DISASTER RECOVERY STRATEGIES
(Dollars in Thousands)

Strategy No.	Disaster Recovery Measure	Preparation Cost	Operating Cost		Priority Level
			Disaster Daily	Standby Monthly	

a. **Evaluating Probability of Occurrence**

1. **Definition of Terms:**

- **Destruction** - Refers to loss from accidental and natural causes (e.g., flood, fire, earthquake), malicious mischief and sabotage. Such events as riot, explosion, erasure of magnetic files, etc., are included.

- **Fraud, Theft and Embezzlement** - Covers the deliberate alteration of data and programs (e.g., modification of tape, disk pack, card files, etc.) plus the removal of physical objectives (e.g., tape reels, check forms, printouts, etc.) Occasionally, disastrous events are planned to cover up such actions.

- **Employee Error** - Includes losses resulting from inadequate procedures or systems design as well as carelessness or indifference by employees. The items particularly susceptible to this problem are data and programs, which can be completely destroyed.

- **EDP Equipment** - This term includes computer main frames and peripherals, plus data entry and related equipment.

- **Installation Facility** - This is defined as the total computer center other than the EDP equipment. It includes the computer and key entry room and library, lighting, air conditioning, wiring, furniture, fixtures, bursters and related ancillary equipment, supplies, forms, tapes, disk packs, punched cards (but not the replacement cost of the data or programs contained in these media) and related support facilities.

Definitions of the other assets is considered to be unnecessary as the terms are self-explanatory.

2. **Instructions for Completion:**

For the Destruction, Fraud/Theft/Etc. and Error columns, identify the probability of occurrence by selecting the appropriate code from the following table. For example, if a high probability for destruction exists for data, enter a "1" in the appropriate box.

3. **Probability of Occurrence Codes:**

1. High Probability

2. Medium Probability

3. Low Probability

The form has space for stating the assumptions made in determining the probability of occurrence. This will point up the critical problems for the study group.

In one sense, filling out this form is an exercise to crystallize the thinking of the Disaster Recovery Planning group and to get them concerned with the more probable problems. It is also used to get a consistent set of multiplying factors in determining the areas of greatest exposure.

b. Evaluating Probable Economic Loss: (Figure 4-15)

  1. Definition of Terms:

- **Without Backup** - The backup facility for each of the categories of assets (e.g., EDP Equipment) either does not exist, does not function, or for any reason fails to provide the recovery capability that it was intended to furnish. For example, assume that the data in the secondary storage facility was totally destroyed along with the data in the regular library. The data must then be reconstructed from source documents as there is no backup file.

- **Current Backup** - The current backup facility provides only the recovery capability that it was designed to furnish. For example, if an agreement with another installation had been made to provide computer time equivalent to 50% of your current work load, assume that the agreement will be honored.

- **Desired Backup** - This assumption represents the reasonable, cost-effective level of recovery capability you would like to achieve. For example, if you currently do not have a secondary storage facility for Data, Programs and Operating System, and Documentation, assume this facility has been created and that the aforementioned materials are fully protected in this storage facility for backup purposes.

  Each of the three levels of backup has three sub-columns:

- **ETR (Estimated Time To Recovery)** - The lapsed time (in days) that it is estimated it will take to fully replace the asset (e.g., data) for a given level of backup.

- **EE (Extra Expense)** - The necessary additional cost (expressed in thousands of dollars) required to continue the normal operations of the business immediately following the destruction of an asset.

- **BIL (Business Interruption Loss)** - The financial loss (expressed in thousands of dollars) resulting from the inability to conduct the company's normal business operations as the result of the destruction of an asset. For example, if a customer order processing system is inoperative because of loss of the programs this event would have an impact on the profitability of the company.

2. Instructions for Completion

The financial loss for EDP Equipment, Installation Facilities, Data, Progams, and Operating System, and Documentation, is to be determined both for Replacement/Reconstruction and for Performance Failure Loss. Estimate the order of magnitude of the financial penalty. It is not necessary to develop a finite calculation when a reasonable estimate can be made. The main purpose is to emphasize the areas of concern, and to put the problems in a financial perspective.

All figures are to be reported in thousands of dollars and are to be determined without consideration of potential insurance recovery.

If the Replacement/Reconstruction Cost, Extra Expense or the Business Interruption Loss is very difficult to calculate, but the sum clearly is of major proportions, the term "catastrophic" may be substituted for a specific amount. The option to use this term should be exercised sparingly.

The intent of the Replacement/Reconstruction Cost portion of the form is to state the costs required to replace or restore the destroyed asset. The cost to regain full operational status when recovery is facilitated by backup resources may be different from the cost to replace or restore the asset without the protection provided by a backup facility.

The intent of the Performance Failure Loss portion of the form is to obtain information concerning the consequences of destruction or loss of all or part of the data processing function including:

- Information on the Estimated Time to Recover to regain full operational status for the data processing function (ETR).

- The Extra Expense that would be incurred in the event of destruction (EE).

- The financial loss that would result from the inability to conduct the company's normal business operations or Business Interruption Loss (BIL).

97

The cost of replacing or reconstructing the several categories of assets (e.g., EDP equipment) should not be included in the Performance Failure Loss section of the form. These calculations have been determined in the preceding two columns, Replacement or Reconstruction cost. This section attempts to determine only the effect of destruction on the on-going performance of the business. Calculation of Performance Failure Loss is to be made under three different assumptions:

- Without backup

- Current backup

- Desired backup

c. Evaluating Possible Costs (Figure 4-16)

1. Instructions for Completion:

- **Replacement or Reconstruction Cost without Backup**
  Identify the costs, expressed in thousands of dollars, to:

  - **EDP Equipment:**
    Replace all existing hardware.

  - **Installation Facility:**
    Completely rebuild or relocate the installation.

  - **Data:**
    Reconstruct all data files from source documents.

  - **Programs and Operating Systems:**
    Write, compile and test all from scratch.

  - **Documentation:**
    Create all flow charts, record layouts, etc., anew.

- **Replacement or Reconstruction Cost with Backup:**
  Identify the costs, expressed in thousands of dollars, to:

  - **EDP Equipment and Installation Facility:**
    Replace all existing hardware or rebuild the installation with no particular time pressure, and with the capability operating continuously.

  - **Data, Programs, Operating System, and Documentation:**
    Become fully operational in each category if a satisfactory secondary (backup) storage site has

been established to house copies of the data, programs, operating system, and documentation.

If there are no clear differences, the figures in the "Without Backup" column can be repeated in the "With Backup" column.

- **Performance Failure Loss without Backup:**
  For these columns, assume that each of the assets has been destroyed, is not available, or does not function because provisions for backup were not made or failed to provide any recovery capabilities.

- **ETR (Estimated Time to Recover):**
  Identify the number of days it would take:

    - **EDP Equipment:**
      For the vendor to replace all EDP equipment.

    - **Installation Facility:**
      To rebuild or relocate the installation at a new site.

    - **Data:**
      To reconstruct all data files from source documents.

    - **Programs:**
      To write, compile, and test all programs starting from the point records are not backed up.

    - **Documentation:**
      To create anew all flow charts, record layouts, etc.

- **EE (Extra Expense)**

    - **EDP Equipment:**
      The overtime costs of clerical personnel, hiring of temporary workers, etc., to perform the entire computer's work load or that portion that could be feasibly accomplished for the time period required to replace the equipment.

    - **Installation Facility:**
      The costs of temporary facilities until such time as the original installation facility is restored.

    - **Data:**
      The overtime costs of clerical personnel, hiring temporary workers, etc., to overcome the problems resulting from the lack of machine-readable data

until at least half of the data files can be reconstructed from source documents. Note that the EDP equipment is functioning during this time period so the cost of "duplicating" the computer work does not have to be included.

- **Programs and Operating System:**
  The same type of costs as incurred for EDP equipment destruction for half the period required to complete all programs, plus the costs resulting from having clerical personnel working with simple listings of data files until half of the programs have been completed.

- **Documentation:**
  The additional costs of systems analysis and programming in changing systems and programs as the result of the lack of documentation for half the time period required to complete the recreation of the documentation.

• **BIL (Business Interruption Loss)**

- **EDP Equipment:**
  The loss suffered from the inability to perform the computer's tasks for the time period required to replace the equipment. Do not consider the reduction in the loss that would occur from the performance of all or part of the computer's jobs by a clerical task force.

- **Data:**
  The loss suffered from the non-availability of machine-readable data for half the time period required to reconstruct all of the data files.

- **Program and Operating System:**
  The same type of loss as suffered for EDP Equipment for half the period required to complete all programs, plus the loss resulting from having clerical personnel working with simple listings of data until half of the programs have been completed.

- **Documentation:**
  The loss suffered as the result of delay in changing systems and programs for half the time period required to complete the recreation of the documentation.

100

- **Performance Failure Loss with Current Backup:**
  For these columns, assume that the backup facility provides exactly the recovery capability it was intended to furnish. If backup for a given asset (e.g. data) does not exist, repeat the data from the "Without Backup" column.

- **ETR (Estimated Time to Recover)**

  - **EDP Equipment:**
    If an agreement has been made with another EDP installation for equipment backup, indicate the number of days it would take to become operational for half of the normal work load. If an agreement for EDP equipment backup for up to half of the normal work load has not been arranged, repeat the figure from the "Without Backup" column.

  - **Installation Facility:**
    Same calculation as the EDP equipment figure above, or repeat the figure from the "Without Backup" column.

  - **Data, Programs, and Documentation:**
    If a satisfactory secondary (backup) storage site has been established to house these three assets, indicate the number of days required to become fully operational for each of them. If a satisfactory secondary storage facility has not been established, repeat the figure from the "Without Backup" column for each of the items that is not protected.

  - **EE (Extra Expense):**
    Given the existing backup capabilities, calculate the additional cost for each of the categories of assets (e.g. data) that would be incurred until a full, normal operating condition has been achieved. Among the costs that might be incurred are the purchase of computer time, travel to and from other computer installations, cost of overtime of clerical personnel, the hiring of temporary workers, and so on.

  - **BIL (Business Interruption Loss):**
    Given the existing backup capabilities, calculate the financial loss incurred as the result of the inability to conduct normal business operations for the period required to achieve the normal operating level. An example would be the profit reduction resulting from the inability to meet production

schedules due to the loss of a portion of the inventory status records.

- **Performance Failure Loss with Desired Backup:**
  For these columns assume that the best possible backup capabilities are available and will function as intended. If no significant improvements can be seriously contemplated, repeat the data from the "Current Backup" columns.

  For the desired backup capabilities, use the same concepts and techniques in determining the Estimated Time to Recover, the Extra Expense and Business Interruption Loss as were used for the "Current Backup" calculations. In filling out the Probable Economic Loss Worksheet (Figure 4-16), use the space provided to identify briefly the "Desired Backup" capability with the associated one-time cost and annual continuing cost.

4.6.2   COST OF MEASURES FOR DISASTER RECOVERY

The costs of measures planned for disaster recovery are best grouped according to the recovery strategies involved and listed in priority order. Management will not necessarily use the cost/benefit ratios of higher priority applications to pay for disaster recovery measures for the lower priority applications. The worksheet given in this section, Figure 4-16, Possible Costs of Disaster Recovery Strategies, is a management summary of the various calculations that have been made for the costs of the various strategies investigated. It is essentially a selection list for management.

Figure 4-16, thus, presents a summary of the possible costs of measures for each disaster recovery strategy and should be summed by strategy. In the disaster recovery study, these costs can be balanced against the possible economic losses, considering the probability of their occurrence. A project budget can then be developed at various levels for approval.

It is important to clearly separate the preparation and development costs from the daily operating costs at the time of a disaster and the monthly operating costs in standby mode.

This cost analysis approach for disaster recovery study is purposely brief. Some of the numbers can be summaries of considerable analysis, while other numbers are simply estimates. In most organizations, however, this level of analysis will be sufficient, as it will be used more for budget purposes than to make decisions on disaster recovery. In general, disaster recovery decisions are made on considered need by management and not on a cost/benefit basis.

4.6.3   INSURANCE COVERAGE

The insurance manager of the organization should be consulted about the insurance coverage on the EDP operations, and the effect on the insurance coverage of the disaster recovery plans. On the one hand, there may be extra insurance needed on the backup sites. On the other hand, a good disaster recovery plan may even reduce the cost of insurance for the organization.

The principle of insurance coverage is to transfer risk of major loss to another organization. Each company or organization will have its own standards as to what risk it will hold internally and what risk is to be transferred.

There will normally be an insurance manager responsible for deciding the degree of risk to be insured. It is the responsibility of the study team to discuss the study with the insurance manager. They should first estimate the possible exposure. They should outline in detail all the equipment, records, and media, stating their replacement cost and actual cash value.

Worksheets are provided in this section to aid this process. These worksheets should be filled out by the study team for discussion with the organization's insurance manager. These worksheets are:

Figure 4-17-1:	Data Processing and Related Equipment (Owned Equipment)
Figure 4-17-2:	Data Processing and Related Equipment (Rented or Leased Equipment)
Figure 4-18:	Records and Media
Figure 4-19:	Extra Emergency Expense
Figure 4-20:	Third Party Liability
Figure 4-21:	Revenue Bearing Data
Figure 4-22:	Business Interruption Insurance
Figure 4-23:	Outside Computer Services

Figure 4-17-1

INSURANCE WORKSHEET

Data Processing and Related Equipment

Owned Equipment

No.	Description	Date Installed	Replacement Cost	Actual Cash Value
1	CPU			
2	Peripheral Equipment			
3	Terminals			
*4				

*List other directly associated equipment

Insurance Coverage on Owned Equipment

Insurance Company	Date of Policy	Policy Amount	Annual Premium	Amount of Deductible

Briefly describe perils named and excluded in the above policies:

Figure 4-17-2

INSURANCE WORKSHEET

Data Processing and Related Equipment

Rented or Leased Equipment

No.	Contract/Lessor*	Date of Lease	Term of Lease	Annual Lease Cost	Lessor** Liability

* If there are several contracts with a given lessor, these may be combined.
** Indicate the extent to which the lessor assumes liability for equipment damage or loss, installed and in transit.

Insurance Coverage on Leased Equipment

If you are covered separately for the difference in conditions if the rental/lease agreement is on a named peril basis and not on an all-risks peril basis, list the coverage.

Insurance Company	Date of Policy	Policy Amount	Annual Premium	Amount of Deductible

Figure 4-18

INSURANCE WORKSHEET

Records and Media

No.	Number and Type of Records and Media	Need or Priority*	Retention Period	Cost to Reproduce	Replacement Value	Extra Expense

*   1. Vital   2. Important   3. Expendable

Insurance Coverage on Records and Media

Insurance Company	Date of Policy	Policy Amount	Annual Premium	Amount of Deductible

Note if the above coverage includes the cost of reconstruction and research if either, or both, active media and source material were destroyed.

Figure 4-19

INSURANCE WORKSHEET
Extra Emergency Expense

No.	Expense	Rate of Expense	Total Per Week	Total Per Month
1	Rental of Temporary Facilities			
2	Rental of Backup Equipment			
3	Rental of Other Equipment			
4	Rental of Furniture			
5	Extra Supplies			
6	Moving Costs			
7	Temporary Insurance Costs			
8	Extra Telephone Costs			
9	Extra Traveling Costs			
10	Overtime Payments to Employees			
11	Additional Employees			
12				
13				
14				
15				
	DEDUCT			
	Expenses Reduced at Original Location			
	TOTAL Extra Expense:			

Insurance Coverage on Extra Emergency Expense

Insurance Company	Date of Policy	Policy Amount	Annual Premium	Amount of Deductible

Figure 4-20

INSURANCE WORKSHEET

Third Party Liability

Note: This worksheet is used only if any service bureau operations or systems work are provided by your organization for outside customers.

Total Sales of Computer Services to Customers $_____

Total Sales of Systems Work to Customers $_____

Insurance Coverage on Third Party Liability

Insurance Company	Date of Policy	Policy Amount	Annual Premium	Amount of Deductible

If you have reciprocal backup agreements with other organizations having similar equipment configurations, include in this list:

a. Coverage for losses incurred to your property by non-organization personnel.

b. Coverage for losses incurred to non-organization's property by your personnel.

Figure 4-21

INSURANCE WORKSHEET

Revenue Bearing Data

Indicate average outstanding balances for a one-year period for revenue bearing data in media form. Specify by type of data.

Average Outstanding
Balance in 19 _____

_____ $_____

_____ $_____

_____ $_____

_____ $_____

Insurance Coverage on Revenue Bearing Data

Insurance Company	Date of Policy	Policy Amount	Annual Premium	Amount of Deductible

Figure 4-22

INSURANCE WORKSHEET

Business Interruption Insurance
(or Loss of Profits Insurance)

Is the coverage under:

    a. Standard Fire Policy?   _____

    b. Data Processing Insurance Policy?   _____

    c. No Coverage?   _____

Explain:

Insurance Coverage on Business Interruption

Insurance Company	Date of Policy	Policy Amount	Annual Premium	Amount of Deductible

Figure 4-23

INSURANCE WORKSHEET

Outside Computer Services

Note: This worksheet is used only if your data processing requirements are handled predominantly by outside computer services.

a. What is the extent of your exposure to damage or loss of data processing media in the possession of outside computer services? If none, explain.

b. Do the service bureaus with whom you contract for services maintain errors and omissions coverage to protect you from loss of profits as a result of their failure, negligence, error, or omission in providing services to you?

If this is in writing, attach a copy.

There will probably be several basic types of insurance policies to discuss such as:

- Property and Casualty Insurance, including Fire, Property Damage, and General Liability

- All-Risk Policies, including Earthquake Insurance, Flood Insurance, and Valuable Papers and Records Insurance

- Business Interruption Coverage

- Extra Expense Insurance

The need for this coverage, or any other special insurance coverage, such as third party liability, business interruption, and so on, should be clearly defined in the discussion. There may be, for example, a considerable business interruption loss which could be insured. However, this is primarily not under the data processing manager's control, and it should be reviewed and requested by the users of the operation, together with the insurance manager.

When data processing equipment is leased or rented, the insurance on it may be borne by the owner. This should be checked in the contract.

The insurance manager will also be concerned that all legal requirements for fire and safety are being met in the facility. Insurance will only be valid if there is full compliance with all fire and safety laws. It is wise to request inspections by both the insurance company and the local fire department. Fire department familiarity with your installation is in itself a useful precaution.

The final decision on the insurance coverage will be determined by the organization policy on such matters. The decision can best be made if the data processing manager first:

- Develops a contingency plan.

- Fills out the worksheets carefully.

- Considers the probabilities of disasters.

The following are brief descriptions of the uses of the attached worksheets:

a. **Figure 4-17-1 and Figure 4-17-2:   Data Processing and Related Equipment Worksheets**

These worksheets are used for listing all computers and peripheral equipment as well as air conditioning and other component parts dedicated to the systems and data processing installation. Include shared facilities, such as air conditioning systems, only if the entire system is dedicated to the data processing installation. If it is shared as part of a central plant unit and insured accordingly, do not include it. Exclude furniture and fixtures, unless they are unique to the EDP function and not apt to be covered under standard property policies. Report gross estimated amounts for the categories. For the purpose of this survey, detailed listings by piece of equipment are not required. However, they may be useful for the Data Processing Manager's records.

Note the following definitions:

- **Replacement Cost:** The cost to replace the property in question with a modern unit in new condition and of equivalent capacity, taking into consideration new materials, technology, and design concepts.

- **Actual Cash Value:** Replacement cost less an allowance for physical depreciation (not book depreciation) and functional or economic obsolescense.

b. **Figure 4-18: Records and Media Worksheet**

This worksheet is for listing all records and media used or stored in the data processing operation. This includes input records, magnetic media records, paper tape records, documentation, printed forms, and stored output.

It can be subdivided into:

- **Active Data Processing Media:** All forms of converted data and programs written on vehicles actively employed in the system. This includes magnetic and perforated tapes, disks, drums, punch cards, etc.

- **Source Material:** All records and data required for the preparation and updating of active processing media. This includes checks, statements, bills, invoices, credit ratings, accounting and service records, etc.

  It is worth listing all types of records or media for insurance purposes. Media vary greatly in importance, however. There should be insurance to cover all media, but in varying amounts depending on importance or need. Media, with the information on them, may be classified as:

- **Vital:** Critical organization information that must be replaced with records in event of disaster.

- **Important:** Part of a regular cyclical processing that may need reconstitution to proceed with the next cycle or to complete the audit trail.

- **Expendable:** Useful information that may possibly be needed, but is far enough back in the cycle so it probably does not need reconstitution. Only the physical tape, disk, etc. will need replacing.

c. **Figure 4-19: Extra Emergency Expense Worksheet**

This worksheet is used for listing the additional cost required to continue the manual operations of the business immediately following damage to systems equipment, media, and necessary source material. Essentially, it is the excess of total operating cost during the restoration period over and above the total operating cost which would have been incurred if there had been no loss. Thus, the amount that the expenses will be reduced at the original location must be deducted.

List all emergency expenses that may be incurred in case of a major equipment breakdown, fire, or other disaster. A few of the possible expenses are listed on the sheet.

d. **Figure 4-20: Third Party Liability Worksheet**

This worksheet is applicable to any service bureau operation, or any systems work, that is provided by your organization for outside customers. Special insurance coverage (errors and omissions) protects the insured against losses experienced by third parties through the insured's own negligence, error, or omission in providing data processing services.

e. **Figure 4-21: Revenue Bearing Data Worksheet**

This worksheet is used for listing records such as accounts receivable, fixed assets, etc., in active data processing media form which are the basis for future revenue claims. If applicable, it should also be used for identification and location of the organization's assets that are leased to customers or used for other revenue-bearing purposes. Loss or damage to such records generally constitutes exposure to losses greater than that of restoration costs or reconstruction.

f. **Figure 4-22: Business Interruption Insurance Worksheet**

The consideration of Business Interruption Insurance, or Loss of Profits Insurance, will depend on the individual circumstances of the data processing organization. If the main product is outside service, this insurance should be seriously considered and the calculation of it will be fairly straightforward. The organization will have income history and projections and will have an idea of the effectiveness of emergency backup arrangements.

If the data processing organization is principally a service group within a larger organization, with no formal payments, the loss of profits must be considered for the larger organization in the event of an emergency. Discussions with the users will yield the type of coverage desired. As the users become aware of the problem of a possible emergency, there will probably be funds available to prepare for the contingency operation.

g. **Figure 4-23: Outside Computer Services Worksheet**

Another insurance problem arises if the organization's data processing requirements are handled predominantly by outside computer services. The data processing media and data are in the control of a third party and there is an exposure to damage or loss that is not covered by the normal organization security measures.

This exposure must be estimated and discussed with the outside computer service. It is important to know if the service bureaus with whom you contract maintain errors and omissions coverage to protect you from loss of profits as a result of their failure, negligence, error or omission in providing services to you. They should also have normal insurance that covers loss or damage to any of your property in their custody.

4.7   RISK ANALYSIS

Risk analysis is the process of identifying and estimating expected losses as a consequence of undesired events. The costs of the safeguards to be implemented to prevent such losses can then be compared to the risks involved. The cost of the safeguard may be limited by the size of the expected losses which would be prevented by the safeguard, unless there are overriding legal or operational requirements that demand the safeguard. Otherwise, the maximum cost of any safeguard should not exceed the expected losses. There are some safeguards, such as fire protection, protection against loss of life, and protection of vital records, which are legally required of management. They may be included in the risk evaluation study, but they will normally be installed, whatever the cost.

Full risk analysis calculations of all application systems and facilities against all possible disasters are very time-consuming and expensive. Organizations which perform any risk analyses usually limit them to critical systems and probable disasters. One of the problems of a risk analysis calculation is that there are a number of assumptions to make and a number of probabilities to estimate. Frequently, management considers that their own good judgment and common sense is just as accurate a way to arrive at the same conclusion. In addition, the pressure of the Foreign Corrupt Practices Act of 1977 has virtually made disaster recovery plans a requirement, and full risk analysis can be skipped.

On the other hand, in a large operation, it is a severe problem to determine, other than analytically, how many of the applications systems will be protected by disaster recovery plans and how rapidly the backup operation need be initiated. Simplified risk analysis calculations can greatly help in these decisions.

In addition to providing a basis for the selection and cost-justification of disaster recovery measures, a risk analysis provides data on time as a factor in assessing the possible consequences of losses. Knowledge of the consequences of not being able to perform each system function for specific time intervals is essential to the creation of disaster recovery plans which will be adequately responsive to the needs of the organization.

With few exceptions, a large percentage of an EDP facility's work load is deferrable for periods of time without causing unacceptable hardship. On the other hand, there is usually a percentage of the work load which must be run because its delay would cause intolerable disruptions. It has proven very difficult to guess reliably and accurately into which category each data processing activity should fall. It is also very difficult to guess very accurately the maximum tolerable delay for the processing of each deferred activity. A properly conducted risk analysis yields this data, which can then be used to justify or reject disaster recovery plan elements based on actual, quantitative needs of the organization for EDP services.

Risk analysis can take a variety of forms. Two examples of risk analysis procedures are given in the FTP Technical Library manual, EDP Disaster Recovery, to determine if the full analytical approach is worthwhile to your organization. Both are adapted from the work of Robert H. Courtney, Jr. of IBM, which was described in "Security Risk Assessment in Electronic Data Processing Systems," June 1978, IBM Corporation. The more complete calculation procedure is from Federal Information Processing Standard 65 (FIPS PUB 65) "Guideline for Automatic Data Processing Risk Analysis," August 1979 (Figure 4-25). An abbreviated version is from the U. S. Department of Agriculture ADP Security Handbook, August 1977. Both of these papers are available from the National Technical Information Service, U.S. Department of Commerce.

MANAGEMENT CONSIDERATIONS

IN EDP DISASTER RECOVERY PLANNING

SECTION 5

RELATED REFERENCES

(Selected by permision from "Quarterly Bibliography of
Computers and Data Processing," Applied Computer Research,
P.O. Box 9280, Phoenix, Arizona)

BOOKS AND REPORTS

EDP Disaster Recovery: Planning, Implementation, and Procedures. FTP, 1981-2 Vols.,
Variable paging. $275.00.

A loose-leaf reference service covering the planning, management, and installation
of an EDP disaster recovery plan. Management and personnel participation in
recovery planning is discussed, and a procedures manual is included. Updated
periodically.

Reed, William P., **Analysis and Design of a Computer Security/Recovery System for a
Relational Database Management System**, NTIS, DEC 82, 239 pp. AD-A124 840/0.
$20.50.

Discusses the design of a computer Security/Recovery System model, its methods
of use, and the advantages and disadvantages.

Security: Data, Facility, and Personnel. FTP. 1982-. Variable paging. 2 Vols.
$375.00.

A loose-leaf reference service written for the internal auditor and/or management's use in measuring adequacy of security in an EDP organization. Planning and
implementation of EDP security measures are outlined. A checklist format covers
both management and technical considerations, including backup arrangements,
company security, insurance, vital records security, physical security, personnel
considerations, software considerations, operations considerations, and data communications. Sections are also included on costs, security hardware and a
bibliography. Updated periodically.

Security Evaluator. FTP. 1980. Variable paging. $125.00.

A loose-leaf reference service designed to measure the adequacy and effectiveness
of an organization's security status. A series of questionnaires are used to evaluate
system internal controls, input and output controls, on-line systems controls, fire
and physical protection, personnel policies, use of outside services, and insurance
coverage. An analysis of security costs is also included. Updated periodically.

PERIODICALS

Ball, Leslie D. et al. **Disaster Recovery Services.** COMP & SEC 1:216-25. NOV 82.

Reviews services of disaster recovery planning vendors to provide fully configured service centers, empty shells, and cooperative arrangements. 19 references.

Batt, Robert. **Lack of DP Contingency Planning Decried.** COMPWRLD 17:19. JUN 27, 83.

Explains that contingency planning in computer operations must be addressed by top management.

Cafferata, O.G. and Lerch, L.A. **Disaster Recovery: What To Do Before the Unimaginable Happens.** CAN DATA SYS 15:38-9. FEB 83.

Describes an approach for preparing against disasters to data processing capabilities.

Defending Your Computer Room Against Disaster. MOD OFF 28:100+. MAR 83.

Contends that a plan is needed to protect data processing facilities from disaster and that a backup procedure is needed to take over when a facility is out of commission.

Friedman, Stanley D. **Contingency and Disaster Planning in the EDP Area.** TODAY'S EXEC. 5:PW5-10, AUTUMN 82.

Focuses on five major issues relating to the development of a sound disaster recovery plan: misconceptions over the scope of a disaster recovery plan; types and levels of potential disasters; disaster recovery plan vs. backup processing plans; contents of disaster recovery plans; and user disaster recovery plans.

Friedman, Stanley D. **Just in Case ...Planning for a Disaster.** SMALL SYS 11:28-31. APR 83.

Focuses on five major issues relating to the development of a sound disaster recovery plan: misconceptions over such plans, types, and levels of potential disasters, backup processing plans, content of disaster recovery plans, and user disaster recovery plans.

Highland, Esther Harris and Highland, Harold Joseph. **A Guide to NBS Computer Security Literature.** COMP & SEC 1:164-76. JUN 82.

Provides a bibliography of special reports and technical studies in the field of computer security that have been published by the U.S. National Bureau of Standards.

Kliem, Ralph. **Disaster Prevention.** J SYS MGMT 34:10-1. MAR 83.

Contends that devastating losses to a company's data processing operations can be lessened or avoided by disaster prevention controls.

Ross, Steven. **Who is the Data Security Officer?** BANK ADMIN 58:52+. OCT 82.

Presents concerns by banks over improper use or disclosure of collected data.

Shaw, James K. and Katzke, Stuart W. **An Executive Guide to ADP Contingency Planning.** COMP & SEC 1:210-5. NOV 82.

Provides the background and basic essential information required to understand the developmental process for Automatic Data Processing contingency plans.

Stoddard, Bud. **Are You Ready for a Data Center Disaster?** COMPWRLD 17:49+. MAR 14, 83.

Contends that major corporations should prepare for data center disasters since the loss of computer uptime or the destruction of programs, documentation, or data films would cripple the organization temporarily or permanently.

Taking "Disaster" Out of Corporate Disaster Recovery. BANKING 75:50. APR 83.

Spells out key elements in a well-thought-out computer disaster recovery plan which include the management role, a team approach, hardware arrangements, software backup, and check and test.

Tuira, Karl. **Disaster Planning Yields Benefits.** COMPDATA 8:25. MAY 83.

Recommends the definition of service level requirements and the availability of shared EDP disaster recovery centers as partial solutions to implementing a viable disaster recovery plan.

Weights, Philip J. **A Methodology for Evaluating Computer Contingency Planning.** EDPACS 10:1-7. OCT 82.

Emphasizes the importance of adequate computer contingency planning based on a disastrous fire which claimed many lives and destroyed a portion of the data processing department.

Wong, Ken. **Quantifying Computer Security Risks and Safeguards: An Actuarial Approach.** INFO AGE 4:207-14, OCT 82.

Defines risk areas and potential losses in relation to computer security and contingency planning. The benefits of carrying out a business impact review are emphasized, and methods of assessing and controlling risks are described.

2

DISASTER RECOVERY
PROGRAM EVALUATOR

PART I

ESTABLISHING DISASTER RECOVERY REVIEW REQUIREMENTS

(Sections 1 and 2)

The review and test of disaster recovery procedures should be based on the business need for those procedures. This part outlines the manual and then provides a self-assessment tool to evaluate potential vulnerabilities in the existing disaster recovery procedures.

1

SECTION 1

HOW TO USE THE MANUAL

SECTION OVERVIEW

This section explains the need for disaster recovery planning and the review of those plans. Experiences of several MIS managers are described. The section then describes the manual, explains how to use the manual in conducting your review, and suggests who in your organization might benefit most from reading individual sections of the manual.

1.1   NEED FOR DISASTER RECOVERY PLANNING AND REVIEW

Contingency planning consists of the advance plans and arrangements which are necessary to ensure continuity of the critical functions of the application systems of an organization. The plans should cover all events of total or partial cessation of operation or destruction of the database or physical facility. Such planning should include procedures, and availability of equipment and personnel for both automated and manual procedures.

The objectives of an EDP Disaster Recovery Plan are to make sufficient agreed upon preparations, and to design and implement a sufficient set of agreed upon procedures, for responding to a disaster of any size in the Information Services area. The objective of these agreed upon procedures is to minimize the effect of a disaster upon the operations of the organization. The emphasis should be on safeguarding the vital assets of the organization and ensuring the continued availability of critical EDP services.

The preparations and procedures should be well understood by the staff. The plan should specify the responsibilities to be handled both before and after a disaster, and document them in a manual which is distributed to, and used by, all supervisory personnel. It should define the basic approach, state the assumptions and priorities, and point up areas of particular concern.

In the event of a disaster in any part of the organization served by the EDP facilities, or dependent on Information Services operation, the plan must be usable on short notice. It must encompass all phases of the migration to, and operations at, the backup sites, should that prove necessary. Sections of the plan must be usable for responses to minor emergencies. After initial acceptance of the plan by management, it must be possible to schedule complete or partial "disaster drills" to activate and test the backup capability.

A "disaster" is any security event which can cause a significant disruption in the Information Services capabilities for a period of time which affects the operations of the organization. It means any situation and leaves the EDP facility in a non-productive state. A Disaster Recovery Plan, then, may also be called a Contingency Plan, or an Emergency Management Plan.

The review and test of a disaster recovery plan encompasses those procedures necessary to ensure that the plan works. Most plans are developed based on a series of assumptions. While the only sure method of knowing the disaster plan works is to have a disaster, it is good business judgment to have that plan assessed in advance.

The review and assessment of the disaster recovery plan should be performed by someone independent of the group that developed it. It is advisable, but not essential, to have that independent reviewer be organizationally independent of the unit that developed the disaster recovery plan. For this reason, many organizations use auditors and/or consultants to evaluate the effectiveness of the disaster recovery plan.

3

1.2   MIS DIRECTORS' VIEW OF THE ADEQUACY OF DISASTER RECOVERY PLANS

Many MIS directors privately admit that their organizations are inadequately prepared in the area of disaster recovery/contingency planning. These same directors observe that in many cases senior management does not have a strong interest in disaster planning, and in many cases is not fully aware of the consequences of a computer disaster in their organization. In addition, only a handful of organizations put much time and effort into reviewing and testing their disaster recovery plans.

Management Information Systems Week interviewed four MIS directors regarding their firm's commitment to disaster recovery, and their assessment of their firm's plan. [1] The four MIS directors are from Coldwell Banker, Standard Oil, Airborne Overnight, and McKenna, Conner, and Cuneo. Their opinions appear to be representative of the current status of disaster recovery planning and the reviews of that planning.

John E. Parady, executive director of McKenna, Conner and Cuneo in Los Angeles, formerly director of information systems for Weyerhaeuser Co.'s 600-person MIS organization, with a total of 20 years in the industry, said he has yet to encounter a company that is adequately prepared for of the loss of a major data center.

"As data processing activity moves from batch to on-line, the backup issue becomes more and more complex," Parady noted. "Most large data centers dealing with large IBM "3033s" and Honeywell "600" tri-processors are finding it hard to have a backup site with the proper mix of hardware and size. The big problem is, however, that MIS has not had a major disaster yet and it may take that to force senior management to take the problem seriously."

In the on-line world, Parady compared the computer system to the cardio-vascular system and said that often senior management looks at it as a "necessary evil."

"How many people can live without a heart?" Parady asked. "Senior management must recognize that companies are more vulnerable than they were before. They know the computer is necessary for business, but they don't understand it; they tolerate it. Another generation of senior management may be required before they try to understand computers. Disaster planning has to fit into the hierarchy of things, into the order of business."

Joseph Barnett, vice president of Gottfried Consultants of Los Angeles, agreed with Parady, stating that there is not an appreciation of the need for adequate backup.

In most large computer user environments, Barnett said, planning is inadequate and understanding of the need is virtually non-existent. Personally speaking, he gave three reasons: the lack of understanding/lack of education about the need, every company's belief that whatever is going to happen won't happen to them, and cost.

---

[1] Management Information Systems Week, Wednesday, April 20, 1983, pp. 1, 26, 27. "Firms Seen Overlooking Disaster Risk" by Velina Houston.

"Contingency/disaster planning should be viewed like one views an insurance policy on one's life or business," Gottfried said. "Fundamentally, there must be an education process before an intelligent decision can be made as to whether or not it makes sense to have disaster planning."

"In today's environment," he continued, "we are looking at the rather substantial cost to the corporation. They weight that against the potential of an occurrence or problem and say they won't bother. Then again, other companies have never even reached a point where they make that kind of decision."

MIS executives, on the other hand, said they believe they do understand the significance of having proper disaster recovery planning and the three executives interviewed noted that their companies' corporate management are in the know.

Coldwell: Very Important: Russell Aston, vice president of MIS at Coldwell Banker in Newport Beach, California, said his company considers the issue very important and has guidelines set up to carry out a full disaster recovery plan. The company has five major data centers located across the country and Aston noted that disaster planning has grown out of the MIS area, but has the full support of corporate management.

"The general guidelines come from the corporate office level and they state that each site will have a disaster recovery plan with certain components involved," Aston said. "The directors of data processing at each site have their own specific plans. Having a backup facility is one of those, and blanket purchase orders with hardware vendors that allow the shipping of a new machine to us if needed in an emergency. At some centers, we have the same kind of equipment so that we can fall to a second center to backup one that goes down."

Standard Oil of California in San Francisco, has had a disaster recovery program in place for many years, according to Bill Zirkle, the firm's standards, security and training manager. He said the corporation has staff working full-time on the program and noted it has existed in several forms and is continually being updated.

"We feel we are prepared in the event of the loss of a data center," Zirkle said, "We are always periodically testing our backup. We have three major data centers and they have the ability to backup each other."

Further, Zirkle said, Standard's corporate management does understand the importance of having a plan. He admitted, however, that this understanding evolved over a long period of time. He said that now support is 100 percent and noted that this communication gap can be a real problem for some MIS organizations.

"We have our plans in place and are adding to and changing our environments," he said. "We try to make having disaster recovery just a normal part of doing business."

Parady agreed about the communication problem between MIS and corporate management regarding disaster recovery. He said the predominant group of MIS directors are "technocrats" who are good at system development, configuration management and hardware, but are "unable to adequately communicate" with senior management. A new breed of MIS directors, he said, is coming of age and these are non-data-processing types who speak "general management language" and are attempting to fit into general management, although he said he felt their success margin was low.

At Airborne Overnight, David Billings, Vice President of corporate systems, said the interest in disaster recovery came from the board of directors and top level management.

He stressed that Airborne's business depends on timely availability of computing resources and that in the last 12 to 18 months, Airborne became serious about developing a workable disaster recovery plan and making arrangements for a full backup site.

"We have recently entered into a contract for an off-site disaster capability with a major vendor." Billings said. "We will be testing the site within the next couple of months."

He said the project is managed out of the MIS area, but said user input is necessary in order to accomplish the task successfully.

"We recognize that MIS can't fully plan recovery without the involvement of the user area and we can't catalog all the things required to do the functions," Billings said. "We can provide the complements of the MIS area and assure their availability in a backup site, but we also require the user area managers to contribute to the disaster recovery planning process."

Barnett agreed that companies must realize how important their data processing capabilities are to continuing business operations. He said Gottfried Consultants works with many financial corporations where a large portion of the business is intimately wrapped up in computer systems and noted such companies can't afford not to have backup.

Parady added that if a large company were to lose a major data center, thereby ruining the continuity of the business enterprise, "business pressure" would be created and data processing or MIS managers would be the ones " 'on the carpet' to ensure it doesn't happen to us."

For Airborne Overnight, Billings noted, cost is a factor in disaster recovery planning only in deciding the level of backup to implement.

Like Standard's current structure or the structure at which Coldwell Banker is aiming, Billings said the ultimate backup is to have multiple data centers each backing up another without severely disturbing its own workload. He added, however, that Airborne is not willing to go to that extreme. Still, he said Airborne is definitely committed to disaster recovery planning.

"We operate an on-line system that supports our field operations on a daily, hourly basis," Billings said. "Not having our systems, even for a few days, would have a significant impact on our ability to do business."

"Our auditors have been pointing out our vulnerability of doing business in terms of our dependency on information processing and our need for disaster recovery planning to support that dependency," he continued. "They made it visible to us, our corporate management and our board of directors."

Barnett, however, said the burden falls on MIS to make sure upper management understands the overall corporate implications of not having adequate backup.

Fundamentally, he said, disaster recovery planning is not a data processing issue, but a management issue.

In pointing out the scenario that MIS environments are quickly writing for themselves, Parady said systems are brought into user environments and are justified by reducing the staff headcount which removes people who have the manual skills to do the job.

Over a period of two years, he said, users become skilled at operating the systems, leaving no one who can do the work manually. The example he used was a system at Weyerhaeuser that supported 30 remote shipping container shops.

"In such a situation, what are you going to do if the system goes down?" Parady asked. "Punt?"

In an effort by MIS executives to apply technology and make it do something useful, Parady said, attention must be paid to the "elegant solutions" needed to run business. Zirkle noted that, after a company has one disaster, everybody - user, MIS, upper management - is ready to jump on the bandwagon.

Parady added the Easterner's proverbial comment which could affect West Coast data centers: "There will probably be a major earthquake in the Southern California area in the eight-point Richter scale range within the next ten years."

1.3   HOW TO USE THE MANUAL

The objective of this manual is to provide a methodology for reviewing the adequacy of an organization's disaster recovery plan. The manual is divided into three parts and six sections as follows:

1.3.1   PART I - ESTABLISHING DISASTER RECOVERY REVIEW REQUIREMENTS

The objective of this part of the manual is to identify the need for disaster recovery, perform a managerial assessment of the level of the concern an organization should have about the adequacy of its their disaster recovery procedures, and then to use that self-assessment as a basis for determining the need and extent of a review program. This material is covered in the following two sections:

Section 1: How to Use the Manual:

This section has described the need for disaster recovery planning and the opinions of selected MIS executives about the adequacy of these plans. This section of the manual describes the manual's extent and contains implementation procedures.

Section 2: Managerial Self-Assessment of Disaster Recovery Programs:

This section describes the major objectives of a disaster recovery program as avoidance of financial loss, meeting legal responsibility, and avoiding business service interruptions. The chapter provides self-assessment checklists for each, obtaining the status of these three major disaster recovery objectives. The result of the self-assessment will be a unique organizational profile for each of the three objectives, evaluating the acceptability of the disaster recovery program in addressing each of the three managerial disaster recovery concerns. The objective of this self-assessment will be to determine the importance of disaster recovery to the organization.

1.3.2   PART II – CONDUCTING THE REVIEW PROGRAM

The objective of this part of the manual is to provide a detailed program for use in evaluating the adequacy of the existing disaster recovery program. The material is designed for use by an independent assessment group. The material is divided into the following three sections:

Section 3: Establishing the Disaster Recovery Review Program:

This section describes a preferred approach and process to review and test the disaster recovery program. The section explains how to create the review team, and then how to build a review program. The section also describes the concerns that a review team might have about a disaster recovery program, as their concerns are basic to establishing the review program.

Section 4: Reviewing Disaster Recovery Controls:

This part of the review is a static review. The section explains how to review controls and then provides the review checklist for use in conducting the review of the disaster recovery controls. This material is basic to understanding a disaster recovery program and to assessing its adequacy.

Section 5: Testing the Disaster Recovery Program:

This section is the dynamic part of the disaster recovery review. It uses testing techniques that in some cases simulate disasters so that the functioning of the disaster recovery procedures can be assessed as they are being performed. Other test processes are more static in nature but designed to simulate in some manner the effectiveness of the test procedures.

1.3.3   PART III – EVALUATING THE DISASTER RECOVERY PROGRAM

The last part of the review is evaluating the adequacy or inadequacy of the disaster recovery procedures. This part explains how to perform that evaluation. It consists of the following section:

Section 6: Evaluating the Effectiveness of the Disaster Recovery Program:

This section provides a methodology for use in evaluating the adequacy of the disaster recovery programs. The section draws upon the information gathered through the process outlined in the previous two parts of the manual. Using this information, the chapter guides the reader in developing an evaluation. Since the only true assessment of a disaster recovery program is the ability to recover after a disaster, the assessment provided by that methodology in this manual will be the informed opinion of the reviewer based on a structured and in-depth look at the disaster recovery program.

1.3.4   HOW TO USE THE MANUAL - BY USER TYPES

The manual is designed to be used by the following four audiences:

- Senior organization management

- Senior DP (information) management

- Computer operations management

- Independent review group

The uses that each of these would make of the manual are outlined in **Figure 1-1, How to Use the Manual - By User Types.** This explains for each of the four entities the pertinence of the six sections of the manual. The primary user(s) is indicated with a P in the column next to each of the six sections, while the secondary users are indicated with a S in the column next to each of the six sections. The use that each of the four audiences can make of the manual is described below:

Organization Senior Management Use: The growing dependence of an organization upon the computer disaster recovery procedures makes concern for and contingency planning absolutely essential. The discussion by MIS directors contained in Section 1 of this manual indicates this concern has not obtained sufficient attention from senior management. Therefore, Sections 1, 2, and 6 might be helpful as a vehicle for orienting senior management to the need for an effective disaster recovery plan, and the importance of the recommendations on how the adequacy of that plan might be determined. The objective of involving senior organization management is to gain their support, both personal and financial, in disaster recovery planning.

Senior DP Management Use: Data processing senior management has responsibility for the adequacy of the disaster recovery plan. In most organizations, the actual development of the plan is delegated to computer operations management. Thus, senior management has the responsibility, but normally does not have the task of developing the plan. The manual can serve their purposes by explaining the need for

Figure 1-1

HOW TO USE THE MANUAL - BY USER TYPES

User Of Manual Section Of Manual	Senior Organization Management	Senior DP Management	Computer Operations Management	Independent Review Group
1. How to Use the Manual	S	P	P	P
2. Managerial Self-Assessment of Disaster Recovery Program	S	P	P	S
3. Establishing the Disaster Recovery Review Program		S	S	P
4. Reviewing Disaster Recovery Controls		S	S	P
5. Testing the Disaster Recovery Program		S	S	P
6. Evaluating the Effectiveness of the Disaster Recovery Program	S	P	P	P

P = Primary User

S = Secondary User

and objectives of the plan. This explanation and the self-assessment results obtained by utilizing the information and techniques contained in Section 2 of the manual will help DP management determine the resources and effort that should be expended in disaster recovery planning. While they probably will not, and should not, conduct the review, the manual will tell them how the review should be conducted, and provide insight into how they should assess and use the evaluation developed under this review methodology.

Computer Operations Management Use: Computer operations management is generally responsible for the development of the disaster recovery plan. This manual will help explain who should be involved in development of the plan, the type of objectives that should be met, and how the plan can be evaluated. The evaluation of the adequacy of the plan should prove to be valuable input in the continuing development of the plan. The manual can also be used to help understand the independent review, and how to use and react to the evaluation developed by that independent assessment.

Independent Review Group Use: A major user of the manual will be the independent review team. The manual is developed to help them conduct the review and develop an opinion on the adequacy or inadequacy of the disaster recovery program. While Section 2 is aimed more at a managerial self-assessment, that section can also prove helpful to the independent review group in determining the type and extent of review that should be conducted in order to achieve the most useful results.

SECTION 2

MANAGERIAL SELF-ASSESSMENT OF DISASTER RECOVERY PROGRAM

SECTION OVERVIEW

This section describes the three major exposures which mandate a disaster recovery program. They are to avoid financial loss, to satisfy legal responsibilities, and to minimize business service interruption. The section explains the objectives of a disaster recovery program, and then concentrates on the three major managerial objectives or concerns about disaster recovery. The section concludes with three self-assessment checklists relating to each of the three primary disaster recovery objectives. The results of the self-assessment is a profile of concern that management should have about each of the three disaster recovery objectives. This profile will help management determine the importance of the disaster recovery program in addressing these three primary objectives.

2.1   OBJECTIVES OF A DISASTER RECOVERY PROGRAM

Security measures are employed to prevent or detect accidental or intentional disclosure, modification, or destruction of data, or the loss of the means of processing data. Disaster Recovery Plans are designed to reduce the consequences of the loss of any EDP resources or capability to an acceptable level. They are not merely planned responses to major catastrophes. They are designed to reduce the damaging consequences of unexpected and undesirable events of any magnitude. The greatest probability is that damaging occurrences will be less than catastrophic, and may be confined to smaller areas of the operation. The size and scope of a disaster and its effect on data processing operations are often not directly related, however. For example, a relatively small fire in the computer communications area could be quite catastrophic to operations, while the loss of some terminals in a completely destroyed building could be recovered rapidly. Data processing operations are so interconnected that there is a need for a Disaster Recovery Plan that covers the whole operation, and any individual parts of it.

Every organization must look at what the consequences of loss of their EDP resources could be and consider their exposure. It is simply good business practice to examine the possibilities of disaster and estimate the exposure of the business in that area. There are three areas of exposure that must be reviewed:

●   Financial Loss

●   Legal Responsibility

●   Business Service Interruption

2.1.1   FINANCIAL LOSS

Because of the efficiency, accuracy, speed, and control of data processing methods, organizations are becoming more and more dependent on their Information Services in normal business operations. The regular, daily operations of large numbers of companies are now completely dependent upon the information flowing from the EDP area. Manufacturing systems, sales and reservations systems, inventory systems, and financial systems, among many others, can no longer revert to manual operations on short notice. An organization's life blood, information, can rapidly dry up if the EDP systems break down. This can cause great financial loss to a company and could even destroy its business if proper disaster planning has not been done.

EDP disaster recovery planning is an action to take steps in advance to ensure the continuity of business information if the EDP capability is lost. It has been estimated that most businesses could survive without EDP for one shift, and probably even one day. By the time three days or a week had passed, however, many businesses would be getting into serious cash flow problems. Within a month without EDP, most businesses would have serious problems of survival. Few modern companies could remain in business today after six months of EDP loss. Large numbers of organizations are highly dependent on their on-line EDP operations to maintain their cash flow.

2.1.2   LEGAL RESPONSIBILITY

Management has a legal responsibility to protect its employees, its corporate resources, and its vital documents. The interpretation of the Foreign Corrupt Practices Act of 1977 has been that officers of a company are personally responsible if there have not been adequate preparations to meet these legal requirements.

It is also clear that officers of a company who have not taken the necessary precautions to minimize the effects of a possible disaster are exposing themselves to legal suit in the event of a disaster which causes losses that could have been reduced. Such suits have already been brought in several instances.

2.1.3   BUSINESS SERVICE INTERRUPTION

The problems of business service interruption do not only include the financial loss discussed above. It also can be deleterious to future relationships with clients. It can affect the public image of the organization for a considerable time. If an organization's business service is abruptly interrupted, for reasons not readily perceived by customers, the long-term effect could be devastating and far more costly than modest preparations for disaster recovery.

If the service is based on a contract with the government, it could well be a contractual requirement that reasonable precautions to maintain the continuity of the service have been planned and taken.

It is simply good business practice to make contingency preparations to reduce the consequences of any security event. Management must be confident that its data processing capability can be depended upon.

2.2   MANAGEMENT REVIEW CONSIDERATIONS

The purpose of EDP disaster recovery planning is to prepare in advance to ensure the continuity of business information if the EDP capability is lost. Thus, disaster recovery planning, particularly as it is being planned and started, is a management rather than a technical issue. It deals with the realities of people, organizational relationships, and special interests. Disaster recovery actions are highly prioritized, and many normal operations are neglected. Management must take the lead and continually assess the technical considerations involved as to their utility.

Some of the considerations for management are listed below.

2.2.1   EVALUATING THE NEED REALISTICALLY

Management must realize that EDP professionals agree there are **no** secure computers. Many computer operations have fine methods for security in place, and management can be assured that the best possible actions have been taken; but there are always people, electronics, and natural disasters that can suddenly disrupt the operations. Management must realistically look at:

- Legal Obligation Requirements

- Cash Flow Maintenance

- Customer Services

- Competitive Advantages

- Production and Distribution Decisions

- Logistics and Operations Control

- Purchasing Functions and Vendor Relationships

- Ongoing Project Control

- Branch or Agency Communications

- Personnel and Union Relations

- Shareholder and Public Relations

Management must assess the importance of EDP operations to these facets of their business, then decide the type of effort that should be put into backup of the EDP function.

2.2.2   PROVIDING ORGANIZATIONAL COMMITMENT

Management must provide organizational commitment to the development and maintenance of a disaster recovery plan. This must include:

- Funding the Planning and Maintenance

- Assignment of Internal Staff

- Obtaining the Interest of Senior Management

- Getting Cooperation from the User Departments

- Involving All Related Departments, such as Security, Buildings, Purchasing, etc.

- Setting Priorities for the Planning

- Reviewing the Planning During Development

- Considering the Use of Consulting Support

- Ensuring Continuing Commitment once the Plan is in Place

- Integration of the Plan in the Normal Business Process

There are three levels of security and disaster recovery measures that should be considered in balancing cost to need. These are:

- Mandatory Measures

- Necessary Measures

- Desirable Measures

There is no absolute scale, and these measures will vary as conditions change. Management must review what is mandatory and necessary for their organization, support those efforts first, and then consider the justification analysis of desirable measures. These measures are outlined below.

2.2.3   MANDATORY MEASURES

Mandatory security and disaster recovery measures are those related to fire control, alarm systems, evacuation procedures, and other emergency precautions necessary to protect the lives and well-being of people in the area involved. Mandatory measures also include those needed to protect the books of account of the organization, and to hold its officers free from legal negligence. The protection must include the assets of the organization insofar as possible. The cost of these mandatory measures must be included in the cost of doing business. The items must also be reviewed periodically as to routine operation and adequacy. They should be reviewed with counsel from the organization.

2.2.4   NECESSARY MEASURES

Necessary security and disaster recovery measures include all reasonable precautions taken to prevent serious disruption of the operation of the organization. This will include selected areas of:

- Manufacturing and Distribution

- Engineering and Planning

- Sales and Marketing

- Employee Relations, and so on.

The necessity of the measures must be determined by senior management, who should also review their understanding of the need periodically. Since the necessary measures will be included in the operating costs of the organization, each selected measure must be reviewed as to both degree and speed of emergency backup required.

16

2.2.5   DESIRABLE MEASURES

Desirable security and disaster recovery measures include reasonable precautions taken to prevent real inconvenience or disruption to any area of the organization, and to keep the business under smooth control. The cost of some precautions related to personnel is small, but planned action is important to maintain operational efficiency and morale. The cost of other measures, such as arrangements for alternate sites for systems and programming personnel and their terminals, may be large. Estimates and plans must be made, however, to allow reasonable and cost-effective management decisions once the extent of a disaster is understood.

The mandatory measures should be implemented as soon as possible. The necessary measures should be implemented in order of priority according to a definite plan approved by senior management. The desirable measures should be implemented as circumstances allow. Overhead cost is balanced against perceived need and desirability.

2.2.6   PLAN TAILORED TO THE ORGANIZATION

An EDP Disaster Recovery Plan must be specific to the organization and tailored to its needs. An off-the-shelf plan is of no use whatsoever at the time of a security event when individuals need to know exactly what their role is and the steps they must take. The presence of a "paper plan" does not in itself provide a disaster recovery capability. All people in the organization who may be involved in recovery should also be involved in the plan preparation, training, and testing.

The disaster recovery planning process can take many months and a great deal of activity and person-days if the full process is carried out in a systematic way, including:

- Review of All Data Sets and Data Files

- Discussion with All Users

- Complete Assembly of All Documents

- Full Risk Identification and Risk Analysis Study

- Detailed Review of Ongoing EDP Security Practices

Such an approach could be self-defeating as it could be very costly and time consuming, and management would lose interest in supporting it. It would also put off the installation of mandatory and necessary security measures that are most critical to the organization.

The better approach for the initial effort is for a small team to gather under the direction of a senior EDP manager and make a short-term, high impact plan to get something in place that will handle the most pressing needs and have high visibility. The steps they should take are:

a.   Assemble all readily available operations and systems documentation.

b.   Assemble the reports of any audits or security studies of the EDP functions.

c.   Create lists of the operating application systems in the first estimation of the order of priority, divided by major organization functions.

d.   Consult with senior management in the financial, administrative, and operational areas to get their opinions as to the mandatory and necessary applications in an agreed order of priority.

e.   Work with Systems Programming and Operations to see that all such systems are backed up at least daily and stored in a secure site.

f.   Determine the minimum configuration on which these mandatory and necessary systems can run (it may be more than one computer) and arrange for tests.

g.   Determine if these critical systems can be backed up and run off-site in an emergency in the time required.

h.   Keep management informed of the results and, when the tests are completed, ask for a full study to be funded to cover all security factors and all applications.

It is important to take less than six months to produce a viable backup capability for the critical systems and do preliminary tests on it. This should have the visibility and impact needed to get support for a more comprehensive study and capability.

2.3   MANAGERIAL SELF-ASSESSMENT PROGRAM

The objective of a managerial review is to provide a macroassessment of the importance of disaster recovery to the organization. The assessment provided later in the manual is a microassessment -- an in-depth assessment of the individual disaster recovery procedures. The macroassessment is done to determine the need for the microassessment.

Let's examine an insurance situation as an analogy to explain the difference between the two reviews. If someone applies for a large life insurance policy they are asked to complete a questionnaire. This is a macroassessment of their insurability. It asks questions like: How old are you; how much do you weigh; what is your occupation; what is the health history of your family; how much do you smoke, drink, etc.? Based on this macroassessment, the insurance company makes a preliminary assessment as to whether or not the individual falls into a high-risk area. If not, the insurance company issues the policy without any additional investigation. In many instances, a representative from the insurance company never meets the individual being insured.

18

The high-risk insurability situation calls for the microassessment. In the insurance example, this is normally a physical examination. The depth and extent of the examination will be dependent upon the degree of risk or concern the insurance company has about the individual being insured. However, rather than spend large amounts of money conducting the physical examination, the insurance company performs the macroassessment first.

The same process is recommended for reviewing disaster recovery programs. Management can make a general assessment as to the degree of the risk they face, and then, based on that degree of risk or concern, they can decide:

1. Whether or not to conduct a microassessment of the disaster recovery program.

2. How extensive any microassessment should be.

The macro, or managerial review, is a risk-oriented review. It does not look at any specific aspect of the disaster recovery program but, rather, looks at the concern management should have over the adequacy of that program.

If the impact due to the disaster recovery is minimal, then that program need not be of importance to senior management. On the other hand, if a disaster in a computer area poses a very high risk to the organization, then management should be extremely interested and concerned about the adequacy of the disaster recovery program.

2.3.1   HOW TO CONDUCT THE MANAGERIAL SELF-ASSESSMENT REVIEW

The managerial self-assessment requires management to look at the organization's business risk due to computer disaster in the following three areas:

- Financial Loss

- Legal Responsibility

- Business Service Interruption

For each of these three business concerns, eight predictors have been identified. In our life insurance analogy we said these predictors were the age of the insured, the weight of the insured, the health history of the insured's family, etc. For example, the age of an individual is a predictor of how soon an individual may die. For each of the three areas of concern, the predictors are used to indicate the degree of business risk faced in that area. For example, in the financial loss area a predictor for the degree of risk is "would repetitive or extended periods of computer downtime add significantly to the cost of data processing?" If the answer to that predictor is yes, then the financial loss risk associated with a computer disaster would be of much greater concern to management than if repetitive or extended periods of computer downtime would not add significantly to the cost of data processing.

19

2.3.2 SELF-ASSESSMENT CHECKLISTS

Management is provided with the following three self-assessment checklists:

- Figure 2-1: Financial Loss Self-Assessment Checklist

- Figure 2-2: Legal Responsibility Self-Assessment Checklist

- Figure 2-3: Business Service Interruption Self-Assessment Checklist

These checklists are to be answered by organizational management (either Senior, DP or both). Each question on the checklist should be answered either yes or no. Some questions are judgmental. In those instances, if management believes the answer is more yes than no, the response should be "yes." On the other hand, if management does not believe that the item is representative of the condition, a "no" response should be given.

If, due to the type of business in which the organization engages a specific item is not applicable, the not applicable (N/A) column should be indicated for that item.

2.3.3 ANSWERING THE SELF-ASSESSMENT QUESTIONS

The following process should be used in answering the self-assessment questions:

Step 1: Select Management Self-Assessment Team

The recommended method to use the self-assessment questionnaires is to have them answered by several members of management including:

- Director of Data Processing

- Comptroller/Chief Financial Officer

- Administrative/Executive Vice President

- President

- One to Three Managers of Areas Dependent upon Computer Processing

The checklists can be answered independently by these individuals, or they can be invited to a meeting to have the checklists explained, and then answered, at that meeting.

20

Figure 2-1

FINANCIAL LOSS SELF-ASSESSMENT CHECKLIST

No.	Item	Responses			Comments
		Yes	No	N/A	
1.	Would repetitive or extended periods of computer downtime add significantly to the cost of data processing?				
2.	Would repetitive or extended periods of computer downtime add significantly to the cost of processing in the areas dependent upon computer processing?				
3.	Would extended computer downtime result in the loss of business for the organization?				
4.	Could financial transactions being processed at the time of a computer failure be lost by the system?				
5.	Could financial transactions be added or deleted while the automated controls are not operational?				
6.	Could all the copies of part or all of an automated file be destroyed in a computer disaster?				
7.	Is the organization liable for any fines or penalties in the event disaster recovery controls are inadequate or fail to recover the system on a timely basis?				
8.	Does the computer disaster recovery plan only include the automated systems and not the financial aspects of operation and recovery of all the related manual systems?				

Figure 2-2

LEGAL RESPONSIBILITY SELF-ASSESSMENT CHECKLIST

No.	Item	Responses			Comments
		Yes	No	N/A	
1.	Are financial assets controlled by the computer systems?				
2.	Do union contracts require that payments to employees be made in a specified time frame?				
3.	Is employee information covered by various privacy laws processed by computer systems?				
4.	Are financial transactions processed by computer systems?				
5.	Are employees subject to danger in a disaster situation?				
6.	Are the only copies of official business records maintained on electronic media?				
7.	Are the only copies of data processing contracts stored in the data processing area?				
8.	Is the documentation supporting the adequacy of computer system controls stored in the data processing area?				

Figure 2-3

BUSINESS SERVICE INTERRUPTION SELF-ASSESSMENT CHECKLIST

No.	Item	Responses Yes	No	N/A	Comments
1.	Would business be damaged if the computer was down for one day or longer?				
2.	Would business be damaged if the computer was down for one hour or longer?				
3.	Has the organization failed to test the full disaster recovery plan to ensure it works?				
4.	Could transactions being processed when the computer went down be lost and not recovered after the computer system was restored to service?				
5.	Can financial transactions that occur during a computer failure be lost and not entered into the system after recovery?				
6.	Are alternate processing methods used when the computer is down so inefficient that customer service is degraded?				
7.	Is the level of security and privacy less when the computer is down than when the computer is operational?				
8.	Are non-data processing employees who use computer systems in the performance of their job unable to continue to perform useful work when the computer is down?				

Step 2: Resolve Inconsistencies Using Delphi Approach

For those items where there is no clear-cut majority for a yes or no response, questions should be asked again. A special checklist should be created showing how the item was responded to by the members of management involved in the self-assessment. If comments were made on any of the checklists, they should be provided back to the respondents. The results should again be tabulated and the process repeated once more in the event that a clear-cut majority (e.g., 75 percent or greater) of the respondents have not answered in the same manner.

Step 3: Tally Results

For each of the three checklists, the number of yes and no responses should be tallied. These can then be posted to **Figure 2-4, Self-Assessment Disaster Profile.** The number of yes responses should be posted as a bar up to the number of yes responses made on the questionnaires. If more than one respondent was used, then the yes responses should be the average number for all respondents.

Evaluating the Disaster Recovery Self-Assessment:

The Self-Assessment Disaster Profile shows the magnitude of the disaster recovery business risk for:

- Business service interruption

- Financial loss

- Legal responsibility

The interpretation of the score of yes answers for each of the three risk areas is briefly described on the Self-Assessment Disaster Profile and described in more detail below:

Score	Self-Assessment	Explanation
0	No concern	Disaster arising from a computer problem does not appear to pose any threat to the organization. It is probably unnecessary to conduct an in-depth review of the disaster recovery program.
1-2	Minor concern	The organization can probably withstand both minor and major computer disasters without any major financial, legal, or continuity of processing threat. A short review of the disaster recovery program may be warranted to confirm that the organization is adequately protected against a major computer disaster.

Figure 2-4

SELF-ASSESSMENT DISASTER PROFILE

"Yes" Responses		Self-Assessment
8		
		Very Serious Concern
7		
- - - - - - - -	- - - - - - - - - - - - - - - - - - - -	- - - - - - - - -
6		
		Serious Concern
5		
- - - - - - -	- - - - - - - - - - - - - - - - - - -	- - - - - - - -
4		
		A Concern
3		
- - - - - - -	- - - - - - - - - - - - - - - - - - -	- - - - - - - -
2		
		Minor Concern
1		
- - - - - - -	- - - - - - - - - - - - - - - - - - -	- - - - - - - -
0		No Concern

Business Service Interruption   Financial Loss   Legal Responsibility

Score	Self-Assessment	Explanation
3-4	A concern	The organization is probably susceptible to a significant threat from a major computer disaster. Most likely the organization can sustain minor computer interruptions without any significant loss or problem. The self-assessment should be made, but can probably be done by data processing personnel or internal auditors. It is probably not necessary to hire a technical consultant.
5-6	Serious concern	The organization is susceptible to a loss through either minor or major computer interruptions or problems. A complete review of the disaster recovery program is warranted. The review should be a high-priority concern of management, and they should take an active role in ensuring that the review is adequately staffed and that the review team receives appropriate management support. The review team should be independent of the data processing area.
7-8	Very serious concern	Disaster recovery should be a major priority of the organization. Loss from a computer disaster is potentially very serious and requires the immediate attention of senior management. Most likely the review should be done by an independent consultant external to the organization in order to attract appropriate attention to the review results.

The management review results can also be used to identify where to expend most of the review time and effort. The above assessment is a disaster recovery objective-by-objective assessment. The three scores can be summarized to develop an overall assessment score. For example, if business interruption had a 6 score, financial loss had a 5 score, and legal responsibility had a 4 score, then the total disaster recovery managerial assessment would be a 5, and evaluated as above.

In addition, when the review is conducted it should be directed toward that objective which scores the poorest (i.e., the most yes answers or highest numerical score). For example, if business service interruption scored a 7, and financial loss and legal responsibility scored 3 each, the bulk of the detail or micro disaster recovery review should be directed at those aspects which relate to business service interruption.

Part II, the detailed review process, is organized by these three objectives. Having managerial direction regarding emphasis, and structuring the program by disaster recovery objectives, should help make the review more pointed and oriented toward answering management's concerns.

PART II

CONDUCTING THE REVIEW PROGRAM

(Sections 3 through 5)

This part describes how to build and conduct a disaster recovery program. The program defined covers both the adequacy of the disaster program controls, and how to test the functioning of those controls.

SECTION 3

ESTABLISHING THE DISASTER RECOVERY REVIEW PROGRAM

SECTION OVERVIEW

This section describes the process of building a program to review the adequacy of the disaster recovery process. The section begins by providing some background material on the areas a disaster recovery plan must address. Using this background and the managerial direction provided when the review was approved, some specific review objectives can be set. Then, a team must be organized to conduct the review. Lastly, the section explains how to establish a plan to accomplish the disaster recovery review objectives.

3.1 DISASTER REVIEW PLANNING

The review process must look at the organization's disaster recovery planning objectives, and then evaluate whether or not the plan is adequate to accomplish them. In order to do this, the reviewer must have a basic understanding of the areas of planning that should be addressed as part of the disaster recovery program. The following discussion describes the type of problems that disaster recovery must address, and the types of planning that are relevant for those problems.

The two situations to which application systems are generally vulnerable are loss of processing availability and damage to data. It follows that the kinds of contingency planning required are:

1. What to do if the network or computing system serving the application is down;

2. What to do if the database becomes so fraught with errors as to preclude further use without compounding the damage.

In both instances, the urgency of the mission supported and of the requirement for system output must be considered. The less delay a system can tolerate, the more extensive the planning will need to be. All plans must be carefully and extensively documented, kept current, and disseminated to all personnel who will be affected by them. Personnel must be trained in their assigned tasks and plans must be tested for feasibility.

The following kinds of planning are relevant for application system emergencies:

Identification of the Critical Functions:

The functions in an application system which are critical to an organization's mission should be identified by performing a risk analysis, which will indicate not only which functions are immediately critical but also how quickly other functions may also become critical.

Alternate Site Operations:

Another organization should be found which uses the same or compatible equipment and, which, during an emergency, would be able to allot time reciprocally. Such an arrangement should be effected on a formal basis between the organizations involved, not left as a friendly arrangement between individuals. Planning should extend to ensuring the readiness at the alternate site of up-to-date, tested software and sufficient preprinted forms and any other special supplies (envelopes, stamps, binders, display devices, storage facilities, etc.) to last through one reorder cycle. In addition, a method must be devised for communicating with the alternate site (telephone lines, messenger, etc.). Adequate transportation facilities may have to be provided and specific personnel must be designated and trained.

Manual Replacement of Limited Processing:

It may be possible that processing of critical functions can revert to pre-automation procedures. Certain types of data are amenable to manual processing for short periods of time; for others, only a severely streamlined version of the function can be accomplished. When continuity is important, any special equipment required for manual operation must be close at hand. Necessary particulars include working space, availability of timely data, page copies of source data, conversion of data to manual use, special equipment, preprinted forms, communications, transportation, selection and training of personnel, and a process for recording all manual transactions.

Backup of Data:

The easiest way to ensure against loss of data is to keep additional copies in readily accessible and secure places. Decisions concerning how many copies to keep, where to store them, and how long to keep them, will depend on the criticality of the application, the vulnerability of the data, and size of the databases.

Recovery of Data:

Sometimes data which has been either accidentally or intentionally modified will be so altered that further transactions will only compound the damage. In such a case, a list of key personnel for each database should be prepared so that they can be summoned without delay when needed. The individuals concerned would probably be senior systems programmers and senior applications programmers. In addition, the list should include the security officer or someone else who could authorize the substitution of extraordinary procedures if necessary, such as access to the computer room not ordinarily granted, access to computer resources not ordinarily authorized, and use of unapproved programs on live data. All personnel who might be involved in such a situation, including the computer operator, should be instructed in emergency measures in advance. Lists of such personnel should be kept up-to-date and should contain names of alternates as well. A priority, based on experience, should be established for checking the source of the errors and a small database should be maintained for testing recovery procedures.

Restoration of the Facility:

If a computer facility is destroyed or damaged, there must be not only plans for continued operation, but also plans for the restoration or relocation of the facility. Recovery from destruction can include locating space or real estate; building or remodeling existing buildings; procuring hardware, supplies, office furnishings, and ancillary equipment; and transferring operations from the emergency site to the permanent one. Such plans will normally be the direct responsibility of facility management but applications systems management may well be called on for support especially in the areas of workload planning, space requirements, equipment requirements and moving operations. Advance preparation and periodic updating of the information necessary to these activities will ensure its completeness and timeliness.

3.1.1   MANAGEMENT CONSIDERATIONS

Even if contingency plans are documented, kept up-to-date, disseminated and tested, and personnel are well-trained, there may still be unanticipated or unfamiliar situations that require an emergency response in a time frame that is difficult. Recognizing this, management should require that personnel who are responsible for security in general, and contingency planning in particular, maintain an awareness of accidents, disasters, emergencies, etc. that have afflicted automated systems in other Federal agencies or private organizations in order to minimize the possibility of similar events occurring at their facilities. The sprinkler system accident which occurred at the Bureau of the Census in 1979 is a case in point. Line personnel responsible for reacting to emergency situation should be briefed on relevant experiences and discussions should be held to ascertain how similar incidents could be handled, should they occur. At a minimum, personnel should be constantly aware of the location and purpose of all emergency control switches.

Management should also recognize that in some situations personnel will not have time to stop and read the procedures. Even well-trained personnel who have been active in periodic testing of contingency planning procedures cannot be expected to memorize all of them. Although it is obvious that more frequent testing will improve employee familiarity with the plan and readiness to handle emergency situations, it is also evident that additional costs will be incurred. One of the major cost-benefit considerations in contingency planning is balancing adequacy of testing against the cost.

3.2   ESTABLISHING DISASTER RECOVERY REVIEW OBJECTIVES

The establishment of review objectives is a three part process:

Part 1:

Determine the types of disasters that can occur. The effectiveness of the disaster recovery program will be dependent upon the type of disaster. For example, the procedures that deal with a fire disaster will be significantly different than that dealing with loss of vital records due to improperly performed procedures. Therefore, the review team must determine what type of disasters are most likely to occur, and then look at the adequacy of the review procedures for each of those types of disaster.

Part 2:

Review the five key areas of recovery for each disaster. Each disaster must address the five key areas of vital records, application systems, hardware/software, personnel, and supplies/facilities. Each of these five areas needs to be evaluated for each type of disaster to ensure that recovery procedures are adequate.

Part 3:

Create review objectives based on the above analysis. Once these objectives have been defined, the makeup of the final review team can be determined and then a review program established.

3.2.1   IDENTIFYING THE TYPES OF DISASTER

No reasonable review program can be created without first reaching an agreement within the organization as to what types of disaster could realistically affect the operation and what are the most probable disaster occurrences to expect. This will be the first major assumption made in developing the review plan. It will be fundamental to deciding the types of reviews that should be conducted.

The various types of disaster to consider include:

a.   **Natural Disasters:**

Floods	Earthquakes
Winter Storms	Hurricanes

b.   **Man-Made Disasters:**

Fires	Burst Pipes
Accidents	Building Collapse
Thefts	Bomb Threats
Willful Destruction	Plane Crash
Sabotage	

c.   **Political Disasters:**

Riots and Civil Disturbances	Strikes
War	Nuclear Attack

This list should be considered by the review team, and the necessary review objectives should be agreed upon. It will depend upon the area of operation of the organization, the location of EDP equipment, and the location of information needs. For example, if the organization's operations are located in a limited geographic area, its disaster response requirements will be quite different than those for national or international operation. A disaster could realistically wipe out the need for EDP operations if it destroyed most of the organization's operations in a limited area. Similarly, some groups will have more concern with earthquakes or hurricanes than will others.

The most likely threats to occur should receive the most attention. These disasters may be localized and preparation for them will be the direct responsibility of Information Services management. Disasters, such as major building fires or hurricanes, are normally the responsibility of other groups in the company as they are generally too extensive for consideration by Information Services people only. Concern for the general organization's operations will then be overriding. The same procedures to back up the EDP facilities should apply, but there will be less concern with the organization's cash flow from the EDP point of view, and far more concern with the protection of the people and the maintenance of overall organization services.

If an organization is widespread, there is considerable incentive to maintain a distant (at least 100 miles) backup site. If an organization is in a narrow geographic area, the backup site could be much closer. In either case, vital records must be kept in a secure place, regardless of geography. The concept of disaster backup sites for vital records is relatively independent of backup operations sites.

Having agreed on the types of disaster to consider, the review team should analyze the most probable disaster occurrences. If this list is of reasonable length, or if the effects of the occurrences will be different, and are readily grouped, a disaster recovery scenario could be written for each type of occurrence, and plans laid for each scenario.

A practical approach, however, is to pick from the list the type of disaster that would be of greatest concern to the Information Services area. This can then be considered in developing the Key Disaster Scenario. Detailed plans could then be laid for it. All other incidents would be considered subsets of the review plan.

Normally, the Key Disaster Scenario will focus on an occurrence involving the computer room, or nearby areas of the EDP facility. This threat would be of particular concern, because it could concentrate in the EDP facility area and not physically affect the rest of the organization. If Information Services is an integral part of the organization's operations, the effect on financial control and cash flow could be disastrous. A sustained shutdown of the EDP facility, while the rest of the organization is trying to operate normally, would be most serious for Information Services management. The Key Disaster Scenario, and the disaster recovery procedures, should be designed especially to meet this threat.

There are five types of disaster to which Information Services operations could generally be vulnerable. (This list may be modified by the Team.) In order of their probability, they are:

a. **Damage to Individual Terminal Areas**

Fire, water damage, bomb threat, or other destruction in a localized situation in a terminal area is the most probable type of disaster to occur. This could be from common causes, such as electric wiring faults or waste basket burning. It would require some readjustment of communications, and the establishment of new terminal facilities, depending upon the priority of the operations involved.

b. **Localized Damage in Information Services Offices**

Similar types of disaster become more critical when they occur in the systems, programming, key input, or support services areas of Information Services. It is likely that such a disaster could affect production schedules, systems development work, or general information distribution. Such incidents could also affect a number of different users at the same time, and records could be destroyed that are difficult to replace.

c. **Damage to the EDP Facilities Area**

Substantial fire, water leak, or bomb threat to areas adjacent to the computer room represent the most likely serious problems to affect Information Services' continued operation. The location of the disaster could be more important than the size of the disaster in this case. A relatively small security event could cripple the whole EDP facility. Damage of this type is uniquely the problem of Information Services management, and is normally selected as the Key Disaster Scenario. Although the most likely problem may be a small electrical fire in a contained area, its effect could extend to all users of the computer services, and the response may have to be complete relocation of the computer operation.

d. **Substantial Damage to the Organization's Offices**

Major fire, major flood from burst pipes, or major bomb or riot threat affecting a large part of the organization's offices may affect the EDP facilities simultaneously. In this case there may be little salvageable equipment or space throughout the area. Organization operational problems would take precedence, but it would be up to Information Services to recover their operations simultaneously. It would probably have a serious effect on the EDP plans, but the Key Disaster Scenario should still be the basis of the activities to be undertaken.

e. **Regional Damage in a Broad Area**

Extremely heavy storms, floods, hurricanes, or acts of war could affect a broad part of the operating area of the organization. There could be widespread loss of power and telephone lines, disrupted public transportation, and substantial difficulty for employees to report to work. If this damage covered most of the operating area of the organization, then Information Services would simply follow overall priorities, and apply its Key Disaster Scenario when it became possible to do so. If this damage was regional, and the organization is national, then the Disaster Recovery Plan would have to include preparations for a major move of all operations to a distant site. That site, and its alternates, should have been selected, prepared, and planned for in detail before the disaster recovery.

The Key Disaster Scenario for most companies need not be concerned with acts of war, such as nuclear bombing, widespread hurricane damage and flooding, or particularly severe winter storms. Such disasters will have such an overriding effect on the company's general operations that EDP recovery will be a minor part of the problems facing management. In such cases, for most companies, Information Services management will probably be able to follow their Key Disaster Scenario after the initial stabilization of the overall situation.

There are a variety of types of possible disaster that can be unique to an industry or a section of the country. These should be considered by the study team.

3.2.2   AREAS IMPACTED BY A DISASTER

The following five key areas of data processing can be impacted by any of the types of disasters that are of concern to the review team:

- Vital records

- Application systems

- Hardware/software

- Personnel

- Supplies/facilities

Each of these five areas are individually discussed below. In conducting this review, the review team should complete **Figure 3-1, Disaster Recovery Review Concerns Worksheet.** This worksheet provides space to document the types of disasters that will be addressed by the review team. For each of the five key areas, the review team should insert in the worksheet the types of concerns they have about each area for each type of disaster. The following discussion should provide sufficient insight to help direct the review team to identifying the proper concerns.

3.2.2.1   IMPACT ON VITAL RECORDS

Vital records are those necessary to ensure the survival of a business. It is important that vital records be given maximum protection from every possible disaster because the information contained in those records may be the single most valuable asset of the organization.   Some vital records are processing and trade secrets, drawings, formulae, and so on. Other vital records are the accounting, operating, and engineering information that is resident on computer media.

Normally, less than two percent of a company's records can be described as vital unless the organization primarily deals with data, such as banking or insurance. In most organizations, a Records Manager, or some other responsible person, has already determined which records are vital and has established a vital records protection program. It is helpful to EDP if this program has included the establishment of a remote, safe storage facility which can be used to store necessary backup tapes and documentation.

In a modern data processing operation, the handling of the records that have been determined to be "vital" is interwoven with the handling of the records that are considered critical for the operations of the mandatory and necessary application systems. The vital records will be classified as "mandatory," and the systems handling them will be given high priority. EDP backup information on electronic media is seldom separated into vital and non-vital categories, however, as backup tapes and disks usually have full application systems on them ready to be stripped out as needed. Despite this fact, the team should be cognizant of which material is "vital" and which is not. They will normally have to assure the Records Manager or the Corporate Secretary that all vital records have been considered and identified and are being given adequate protection.

Figure 3-1

DISASTER RECOVERY REVIEW CONCERNS WORKSHEET

Type Of Disaster	Areas Impacted By The Disaster	Vital Records	Application Systems	Hardware Software	Personnel	Supplies/ Facilities

In general, the measures that are taken to assure the general efficiency of the computer and its use by the company, and to back up mandatory and necessary systems, are identical to those measures that should be taken to protect vital data processing operations. It is sufficient for the team to identify the vital records, then treat them in the "mandatory" class of backup and recovery handling.

Records Retention Analysis is related to vital records requirements because its prime legal use is for the vital records. It should be extended to all data processing records, however, because of its usefulness in keeping some control on the volume of retained data. There are three types of retention purposes. These are (see **Figure 3-2, Records Retention Periods**):

1. **Legal Retention:** The period of time required by such agencies as the IRS and the Interstate Commerce Commission. These required records become vital records.

2. **Processing Retention:** The period of time specified in the Operations Manual as necessary to restart the processing of that data in the event an error is detected subsequent to initial processing.

3. **Disaster Retention:** The storing of necessary data on a computer media that facilitates off-site storage on a cyclical basis sufficient to resume normal data processing activities in the event of a disaster at the computer site.

3.2.2.2   IMPACT ON APPLICATION SYSTEMS

Application systems requirements must be determined individually and in detail before any priorities are set and assessments are made for the disaster recovery planning. The review team must discuss individually, with each systems analysis group, the details of each application system and their view of its priority. Discussions should then be held with the user contacts to get their views of the availability requirements and the priorities of the system.

    a. **Application System Service Availability Requirements:**

For the purposes of discussion and analysis, the team can use **Figure 3-3, Application System Service Availability Requirements** to get a first understanding of what the disaster recovery needs will be. For large application systems, groups of programs may be used to subdivide the entries. Rough estimates are acceptable on the first review of the application. The columns of Figure 3-3 are:

Application Systems: Names of systems, groups of programs, or individual programs, as is reasonable.

Report Frequency: For batch reports. Response time for on-line.

Figure 3-2
(Page 1)

RECORDS RETENTION PERIODS

A. Records With Retention Periods Specified By Government Regulation

Type of Record	Retention Period (Yrs.)	Type of Record	Retention Period (Yrs.)
Accounting & Fiscal		**Purchasing & Procurement**	
Accounts Payable Invoices	3	Bids and Awards	3
Checks, Payroll	2	Purchase Orders & Reqs.	3
Checks, Voucher	3		
Earnings Register	3	**Security**	
General Ledger Records	Permanent		
Labor Cost Records	3	Employee Clearance Recds.	5
Payroll Registers	3	Visitor Records	2
Manufacturing		**Taxation**	
Bills and Material	3	Annunity and Other Plans	Permanent
Engineering & Specs. Records	20	Dividend Register	Permanent
Stock Issuing Records	3	Employee Taxes	4
		Excise Reports	4
Personnel		Inventory Reports	Permanent
		Depreciation Schedules	Permanent
Accident Reports & Claims	30		
Changes and Terminations	5	**Transportation**	
Injury Frequency Records	Permanent		
Job Ratings	2	Bills of Lading	2
		Freight Bills	3
		Freight Claims	2

Figure 3–2
(Page 2)

RECORDS RETENTION PERIODS

B. Typical Records With Retention Periods Fixed By Administrative Decision

Type of Record	Retention Period (Yrs.)	Type of Record	Retention Period (Yrs.)
Accounting & Fiscal		**Manufacturing**	
Accounts Payable Ledger	Permanent	Production Reports	3
Accounts Receivable Ledger	5	Work Orders	3
Bank Statements	3		
Budgets	3	**Personnel**	
Expense Reports	3	Attendance Records	7
Financial Statements, Cert.	Permanent	Employee Activity	3
P & L Statements	Permanent		
Commission Reports	3	**Plant Records**	
		Inventory Records	Permanent
Corporate		Maintenance	5
Capital Stock Ledger	Permanent	**Taxation**	
Stock Transfer Records	Permanent	Tax Bills & Statements	Permanent
		Tax Returns	Permanent

Note: The above Retention Periods are given as typical examples. In practice, an organization must determine its own Records Retention Periods.

Figure 3-3

APPLICATION SYSTEM SERVICE AVAILABILITY REQUIREMENTS

Group or Division _____

Application System	Report Frequency	On-Line Or Batch	Areas Of Exposure	Unacceptable Period Of Loss Of Availability	Potential Losses	Other Considerations

On-Line or Batch: If both, separate the line entries.

Areas of Exposure: Legal requirements, financial, customer service, public relations, etc.

Unacceptable Period of Loss Availability: Start with the user's statement about acceptability of any disruption. Discuss later.

Potential Losses: Give initial estimates for hour, day, week, and month, if applicable. If a risk analysis is made, these numbers will be refined for specific systems.

Other Considerations: Mention Foreign Corrupt Practices Act, if applicable, and any senior management directives.

It will be useful to develop an Application System Service Availability Requirement form for nearly all application systems, even those of low priority in the first analysis. Clearly, low priority systems need not have the same level of analysis in detail as the higher priority systems.

b. **Application Systems Priority:**

After all application systems have been identified and some information has been gathered about them, the team should discuss their priority with senior management. All application systems in each group or division of the organization should then be ranked in priority sequence according to the desires of the management of that group or division. (See **Figure 3-4, Application Systems Priority.**)

It is not necessarily simple to assign a rank order or priority to all systems, so the effort should be put into ranking the "Top Five" (or other number as seems reasonable) and then giving only an approximate priority to the remainder. After the application system priorities have been agreed upon in each group or division, the team must then discuss with senior management how to assign relative priorities to the different groups so that an overall priority list can be developed. This is usually not difficult as it is fairly obvious which are the top priority systems in an organization. The columns of Figure 4-3 are:

Priority: Firm listing of the "Top Five" as discussed and approximate listing of the remainder.

Application System: Name of system or groups of programs within a system.

Systems Contact: Name of lead systems analyst for the system.

Figure 3-4

APPLICATION SYSTEM PRIORITY

Group Or Division _____

Priority	Application System	Systems Contact	User Contact	Basic Processing Reqmts.	Report Frequency	Minimum Terminal Reqmts.	New Development?	Comments
Top Five								
1								
2								
3								
4								
5								
Approx.								
6								
7								
8								
Etc.								

User Contact: Names of working systems contact, plus user manager involved with the system operation.

Basic Processing Requirements: Computer, memory used, and the operating system used.

Report Frequency: For principal reports. Note if on-line for reports, data entry, or both.

Minimum Terminal Requirements: Type of terminals and minimum number that would be needed in disaster recovery.

New Developments: Note if any substantial modification or development is presently being undertaken on the system.

Comments: Management requirements, special requirements, etc.

3.2.2.3 IMPACT ON HARDWARE/SOFTWARE

a.   Hardware Requirements:

Hardware resources are usually readily replaceable if the equipment is of recent manufacture and is produced in sufficient quantity for the manufacturer to have replacement devices ready to ship on short notice. The policy of most hardware manufacturers is that, in the event of a localized disaster, the customer will be moved to the front of the line for shipment of replacement units that are avavilable. Some CPU's may require a larger, more modern one shipped because the other is no longer in production. For other units, the vendor may ship one that they are using for demonstration. In any event, most hardware vendors are prepared to give the most rapid replacement service possible. Their engineers will normally work around the clock to bring up the needed system. There are some differences between various vendors, however, and agreements or understandings should be obtained well in advance of problems occurring. Only a few of the vendors will put detailed agreements in writing, but experience has shown that the great majority will put forth a "best effort."

Those EDP installations that have multiple-vendor, mixed equipment, must be aware that each vendor will normally supply only replacements for its own equipment if the replacements are coming out of their delivery line. Otherwise, they could have legal difficulty with their other customers.

There are a number of hardware devices that may be quite difficult to replace rapidly in an emergency. These include:

- Equipment which has a complex array of optional features and has been effectively customized for the application. Complex communications controllers are an example.

- Equipment manufactured in small quantities or on demand. Large memory arrays are an example.

43

- Equipment which is application sensitive, such as check sorters.

- Equipment that is obsolete or becoming obsolete.

- Equipment manufactured by companies no longer in existence. The used equipment market should be searched for replacements.

The ease of replacement of hardware is usually a secondary consideration in disaster recovery planning because manufacturers are attuned to giving emergency aid. At a very minimum, it still takes 24 to 48 hours to get replacement hardware, however, and then it has to be tested and brought up. Frequently, deliveries take several days. Therefore, if there are functions that need immediate backup access, the backup hardware to be used must be already in place and operating at an existing site. This could be your own equipment, equipment available through agreements with others, or commercial installations. The actual details must be carefully arranged in this stage of the disaster recovery preparations.

b.   Communications Requirements:

The size and complexity of the communications network supporting an EDP facility is a major factor in contingency planning. The dependency of time-critical functions must be understood in detail before steps can be planned to provide backup and recovery. The Telephone Company normally responds very rapidly in restoring communications lines. The problem lies in restoring sufficient numbers of terminals, modems, controllers, etc., and in adjusting the systems software to recognize the new configuration from a new computer and a new location. It may be necessary to change local operation to remote and vice versa. Clearly, the systems programming problems are considerable and require careful planning if rapid recovery is a necessity.

Common carriers have available the means to switch leased telephone lines under remote customer control from the initial termination to alternate sites. The switch, the controllers, and the lines are all tariffed separately and may even be supplied by separate vendors. The complications are obvious, but the rapid switching of many lines may be economically feasible if the organization's dependency on them is great. This must all be reviewed in the preparatory analysis. If there is careful planning, the greatest problem will still be in the development of the required systems software to exactly meet the new configuration.

Clearly, if the importance is sufficient, the capability must be developed to route all communications to each of two (or more) sites. With this alternative, there can be a rapid changeover from a damaged site to the backup. The economic feasibility and the time dependencies must be analyzed carefully to determine the necessary approach to communications backup.

c.   Software Requirement:

Systems software and application programs are a special case of data handling. In fact, most backup tapes simply group all machine-readable data together. In time of emergency, it is then the problem of Systems Programming to strip out the various meaningful groups of information.

Software programs tend to have a greater stability than data, but they are sufficiently subject to change that care must be exercised to assure that fully current versions, and all documentation, are sufficiently protected.

Application programs can be particularly vulnerable in EDP operations if there is not careful management attention to the use of development disciplines and change control. Formalized program management procedures are necessary to be assured that programs can be rapidly backed up. If an author/programmer is in any way needed to keep normal operations going, it will be difficult to have a workable contingency plan.

One of the critical disaster recovery preparations that is required is to work out formal agreements with the vendors of any licensed program packages that are used. The copying of these is generally forbidden in the contract, so it is up to the vendor to maintain the ready availability of replacement copies. They should be prepared to state from where replacement copies will be shipped, how soon they could be expected after a security event, and whether they will have personnel available to give support to the recovery process.

d.   **Power and Environmental Systems Requirements:**

Uninterruptible Power Supply (UPS) systems normally fulfill the useful function of protecting against power line transients and other brief interruptions, and thus keep the system running smoothly with fewer restarts and less potential damage to data integrity. They also provide a short period during a primary power failure, during which a standby generator can be brought into operation to support the critical data processing functions. They further provide a useful function in the case of many types of disaster. They provide a short period, usually from fifteen to thirty minutes, during which the system can be brought down gracefully without loss of information.

It has been pointed out that power and environmental control systems are the most expensive and time-consuming to bring up at a new site. No reasonable backup can be expected unless the emergency site has been well-prepared in advance with such equipment.

3.2.2.4   IMPACT ON PERSONNEL

Personnel are the most critical resource of any EDP organization. Recovery from damaging losses is highly dependent on the availability and participation of knowledgeable, experienced personnel. People provide the flexibility, availability, and versatility needed to meet an unexpected situation and to adapt the previously made plans to the situation as it actually exists. It is, therefore, necessary that all personnel who are to be involved in a recovery plan have studied the plan, have been trained in its execution, and have been given an opportunity to suggest changes and additions.

People can be expected to innovate, perform unfamiliar tasks, work under stress, and work long hours if they feel that they are a part of the plan. For a successful recovery operation, belief in the inherent importance of the organization's mission must have been instilled previously to motivate the staff to carry out the work under stress. The planners of a backup and recovery operation must consider whether the EDP facility operates in a way that dependence can be placed on the staff in unusual situations.

Preparations will be different for the handling of personnel dealing with a localized fire or minor disaster as compared to those dealing with a regional disaster, such as extreme weather conditions, floods, hurricanes, tornadoes, etc. It must be constantly remembered that the safety of personnel is of paramount importance, and this will include the safety of their dependents when there is regional danger.

a. **Planning Personnel Actions:**

The planning of personnel actions, moving between sites, possibly crowding into offices and handling unfamiliar tasks, must be carefully considered in detail. People should be informed in advance where they will be expected to report, how they will get there, and what their additional responsibilities will be. In preparation for such moves, it may be necessary to examine floor plans in detail, to have some extra equipment available, to lay in heavier electric power lines, more standby telephone lines, and so on, to be assured that when the people are moved, they will be able to work effectively.

If two or more sites routinely provide backup to each other during periods of equipment changeover, scheduled maintenance, or minor failure, the personnel will become familiar with the operation. It will essentially be a continued rehearsal of a disaster situation. In such cases, the people involved should understand the problems of emergency recovery in detail and should be able to make worthwhile suggestions for the plan.

b. **Telephone Trees:**

Part of the preparation for disaster recovery is assembling the names, addresses, and telephone numbers of all persons who may be involved. This is not necessarily as simple as it sounds as many personnel departments do not release telephone contact information for employees. They consider that home addresses and telephone numbers are confidential information which should not be written down and distributed widely where they can be used for someone else's commercial gain. There is a simple way of circumventing this problem, which must be carefully worked out in advance. Do not publish a single, comprehensive "telephone tree," but merely publish the telephone numbers of the key contacts and their alternates. They, in turn, will have lists of the people they should call, and so on.

c. **Training:**

People must be given sufficient training in the problem being considered, the reason for the plan structure, and their parts in it. This must be training with feedback that is repeated periodically or when there is a change of staff. They must rehearse their roles to the extent necessary and be provided with any skills training that may be required.

Each person must be recognized as an important link in the overall plan. Since most people involved will be quite experienced in their own special areas, they should have their suggestions considered seriously.

One possibility to consider is to offer positive rewards for any outstanding performances during emergencies. This would serve to advise all personnel of the special nature of their activities during and after a security event.

3.2.2.5 IMPACT ON SUPPLIES/FACILITIES

Most supplies are catalog items with reasonable availability. Most facilities have a sufficiently large number and variety of such items to make plans for stockpiling needed at more than one location. Valuable time can be lost, however, if supplies are not carefully cataloged and analyzed. The stores people must be told what will be needed in the event of an emergency.

Paper stocks and forms are obviously the critical area to analyze because many of the forms may be special and very large quantities of some forms may be routinely used. Adequate buffer supplies of stocks should be kept in two or three locations. Vendor information should be available in an emergency for the critical stocks. Many office supplies are available on the open market locally and need not be backed up to any great extent.

A strong forms control program can be invaluable in a disaster situation. All forms will be adequately cataloged, with samples, and the information will be available at more than one site. This is most important with specially-printed forms and internally developed forms.

The provision of supplies is not a minor task and must be integrated into the recovery program. Most supplies are stored in basements or near vulnerable areas and, by the nature of paper, they are particularly susceptible to water damage, be it from storm floods or firemen's hoses.

Particular care must be given to the identification and continued availability of critical items in stock and of special forms on which there may be critical dependence. The replacement lead time of such items can be great if adequate backup stocks have not been arranged.

a.   Transportation Requirements:

There are two transportation problems to be considered in disaster recovery preparations. One is the effect of a regional disaster on public transportation and the ability of employees to get to work and deliveries to be made. The other is the rapid movement of people and supplies to an alternate site and the regular "shuttling" between sites during the security event.

Events which disrupt the transportation of people and supplies over a region cannot be readily overcome and present a serious obstacle to the effective operation of the EDP facility. Even overnight accommodations nearby will be difficult to obtain because of the competition for them. Such problems as a widespread power failure, earthquakes, labor difficulties, riots, and so on, can generally only be met by locating the backup facility at a considerable distance from the affected facility, and depending upon other personnel to operate it.

If the disaster is localized to the EDP facility, however, and an operating backup site is available within 50 miles, a different set of plans should be prepared. In this case, some personnel will be expected to use their own cars and commute in a different direction. Others will be helped by using public transportation in a different way. Still others, who may normally walk to work or share in ride groups, will need to have shuttle buses arranged from convenient pick-up sites. Plans will have to be made for rapidly renting such buses or vans, getting drivers, and making the schedules known. A number of smaller vehicles may also have to be arranged to move critical personnel and supplies from site to site routinely. Still other arrangements may have to be made to take vans with snacks and drinks to the new site. All such contacts should be made in advance with lists of vendors, telephone numbers, costs, etc., prepared.

b.   Facility and Office Space Requirements:

There are two possible objectives in the selection of space into which an EDP facility can be moved after the loss of an original site. They are:

1. Space which can be used temporarily until the original site is restored.

2. Space into which the EDP facility can relocate with relative permanence.

A move from a damaged site to a partially prepared floor space cannot be done rapidly. Cooling water, air conditioners, raised floors, and the like are time-consuming to install. It may take several weeks if environmental equipment is to be acquired. Site preparation must be done in advance, if recovery is needed on the same day as the loss of capability or very rapidly. Communications lines, power lines, and ancillary environmental equipment to support the critical functions must be installed well before a problem occurs. Such work is expensive, however, and should not be undertaken unless the need for rapid backup is great or if the site could be used regularly for taking part of the normal data processing load. Plans for space into which the facility can be relocated should therefore reflect, whenever possible, the future growth plans of the organization.

A major consideration in plans for backup space for the computer complex is the ability to provide simultaneous office space for terminal users and other staff on a local basis. Local operations are considerably less complex than remote operations.

c.   Documentation Requirements:

All backup documentation should be analyzed so that needed material is available at the off-site facility in time of need. The best approach for backing up operations documentation and systems programs is to use one of the several word processing or similar library systems available and have all the information in machine-readable form. It can then be routinely backed up with other data and taken to the backup site. There it can be stripped out if needed.

The greatest problem comes from user manuals, system manuals, program manuals, etc. These tend to be given narrow distribution and kept in fire-prone areas such as paper-cluttered offices. One approach is to put them on a library control system and store backup copies at a remote site. However, they then tend not to be updated correctly over time. Another approach is to microfilm all such manuals, at least annually, and store in a secure place. This can be more expensive. The problem of backing up documentation must be studied carefully in the plan preparation phase, even though it is not generally a popular activity.

Of special consideration is the backup of the Disaster Recovery Plan itself. Since it will have details of names, phone numbers, contacts, equipment inventories, alternate site agreements, and so on, that cannot be readily memorized, copies of the Plan must be available immediately at the time a disaster is recognized. This means that copies of the Disaster Recovery Procedures (the Action Plan) must not only be distributed to key locations in the EDP facility and the Information Services offices, but they should also be kept at the homes of the key people who will be contacted in time of emergency.

There are two reasons for keeping copies of the Disaster Recovery Plan at the homes of key individuals. The first is that a serious disaster could keep people from entering the facility and offices. The second is that most serious fires start at night or weekends. If a fire starts during the working day, it is normally detected quickly, and handled. The same applies to water and steam leaks, and break-ins.

3.3   BUILDING A REVIEW TEAM

The review of the disaster recovery plan can be performed by either an individual(s) from a single organization, or by a review team. We will look at the advantages and disadvantages of each, and then make up a review team.

The advantages of an individual(s) from a single organizational unit conducting the review include:

- Less coordination

- Normally the review is shorter in duration

- Easier development and agreement to review report

- If individual has appropriate credentials, the opinions may carry more weight than that of a group of lesser respected individuals

- The cost of the review may be less

The advantages of a review team include:

- The synergistic effect of multiple disciplines applied to the review

- Better acceptance of the review recommendations from the areas represented on the review team

- Potentially a more thorough review because more individuals are involved

- More pressure placed on management to accept the review recommendations because of the wide divergence of areas represented on a review team

When an individual(s) from a single area conducts the review, the types of reviewers can include:

- Internal auditor

- External auditor (e.g., CPA)

- Disaster recovery consultant

- Internal specialist in disaster recovery (probably from computer operations)

When a team is selected, the recommended makeup of the team includes individuals with the following background/representation:

- Representatives from key user areas

- Representatives from the area responsible for managing the building

- Organization security unit

- Organization's information security unit

- Legal department/legal counsel

- Purchasing/procurement

- Internal audit

- Senior management

- Data processing management

- Chairman of the disaster recovery task force/committee

The selection of the disaster recovery review team or individual should be made by the organization's senior management. Note that in many instances, the recommendation will come from the manager responsible for disaster recovery, but should be approved by senior management to ensure its involvement and support of the review process. In those instances where the review is initiated by the audit function (and sometimes the security function), senior management may not be directly involved in the initiation of the review, but will have been involved in the approval of the internal audit, or security annual review program.

3.4 CREATING A REVIEW PROGRAM

Prior to commencing the on-site disaster recovery review, a work program should be created. This work program should be designed around the concerns identified in Figure 3-1. Each concern that the review team believed represented a significant threat to the organization should be reviewed.

The disaster recovery review program is a blueprint for the review team. When all of the identified significant disaster recovery concerns have been assessed, that concern, the review is complete. Using this process, the review is more structured, will be directed at specific problems, and it can be determined when the review is finished. It also provides the basis of identifying to management the scope of the review, and becomes the basis for developing an evaluation and opinion of it.

Normally, the disaster recovery review program is developed by the senior members of the review team. It is recommended that the program be reviewed by the entire team before finalized. It is necessary that the review process be developed to the extent that specific objectives or tasks can be assigned to individuals, and they can be instructed on the type of test that they should perform in order to complete the task and/or satisfy the review objectives.

A worksheet for documenting the disaster recovery review program is provided as **Figure 3-5, Disaster Recovery Review Program.** The information that needs to be recorded on this worksheet, together with the process of gathering that information, is described below:

No. (#): A sequential number of disaster recovery concerns/review objectives to be accomplished.

Disaster Recovery Concern: Each of the concerns identified on Figure 3-1 that are significant to the review team should be transcribed to this column. The concerns should be sequentially numbered or cross-referenced back to the appropriate intersection on Figure 3-5.

Objective Impacted: Financial (Fin.); legal responsibility (Legal); business service interruption (Svc.) - Each of the concerns should be evaluated to determine whether they are related to a financial loss, legal responsibility, or interruption of business service. A checkmark should be placed in the appropriate column(s).

Review Objective/ Task: The objective task to be accomplished to determine whether or not the concern has been adequately addressed by the disaster recovery program should be indicated here. For example, if the concern for the man-made disaster of fire, for hardware/software, is that there is inadequate resources to extinguish a fire shortly after is is ignited, then the review objective/ task might be to evaluate the fire detection system and correct the process to ensure it is adequate to quickly put out a fire.

Figure 3-5

DISASTER RECOVERY REVIEW PROGRAM

#	Disaster Recovery Concern	Objective Impacted			Review Objective/Task	Assigned To	Type Of Review		Comments
		Fin.	Legal	Svc.			Static	Dynamic	

Assigned To:	The individual member or members of the review team who are to accomplish the indicated objective or task should be identified. If only a single individual is performing the review, this information need not be completed on the worksheet.
Type of Review: Static or Dynamic:	A determination should be made as to whether the test will be static (the assessment will be made on the merits of the documented disaster recovery program) or the test will be dynamic (the test will evaluate the effectiveness of the executed disaster recovery process). Note that in some instances dynamic tests may not be practical, such as in the previous example of testing the fire-extinguishing equipment.
Comments:	Any suggestions, constraints, or limitations that will be helpful to the individual assigned to accomplish the review objectives/task can be indicated in the comment column. In addition, specific tools for conducting the test may be indicated. Note that if the comments are extensive they can be documented on a separate sheet and cross-referenced in the comments column.

SECTION 4

REVIEWING DISASTER RECOVERY CONTROLS

SECTION OVERVIEW

This section provides the methodology and worksheets to review the disaster recovery program controls. The use of these checklists comprises a static review of the disaster recovery program. The review looks at the completeness of the disaster recovery program as a basis of controlling the financial losses, legal responsibilities, and loss of service associated with a computer disaster. The checklists address each of these three major objectives, and are organized into the five impacted areas of vital records, application systems, hardware/software, personnel, and supplies/facilities. The results gathered through the execution of these checklist review programs will be used in developing an opinion as to the adequacy of the disaster recovery program.

4.1 PROCESS FOR REVIEWING DISASTER RECOVERY CONTROLS

The disaster recovery program is a control against loss associated with a computer-oriented disaster. Therefore, by definition every aspect of the disaster recovery program is a control. Thus, the review will be assessing what is within the existing program and will seek possible omissions that might impact the effectiveness of the program.

The primary purpose of controls is to reduce the probability of loss by realization of a threat. Proper evaluation of the adequacy of disaster recovery controls becomes a three-step process as follows:

Step 1: Identify Disaster Recovery Concerns

The concerns to be reviewed have been identified in Figure 3-5. These are the concerns or risks that are of significant enough magnitude that they require controls. Thus, these concerns scope the areas or risks in which the disaster recovery controls will be evaluated.

Step 2: Identify The Controls In Place That Will Reduce The Concerns

For each identified concern, the review team must identify the controls which can help reduce the loss generated by that concern or threat. Note that a single control may be helpful in reducing the loss associated with more than one concern. Therefore, when a control has been identified the review team must determine all of the concerns that that particular control can be beneficial in reducing.

Step 3: Assess The Adequacy Of Controls

The adequacy of control is like a scale. On one side of the scale is the magnitude of the concern, and on the other side of the scale is the strength of controls. If the controls are equal to the magnitude of the concern, the review team can conclude that the controls over that concern are adequate. On the other hand, if the magnitude of the concern is greater than the controls then the controls will be considered inadequate; and if the controls are greater than the magnitude of the concern the controls can be considered more than adequate. Figure 4-1 should be used to determine the adequacy of controls. Note that the checklist provided in the latter part of this section should be used to identify the controls.

4.1.1 COMPLETING THE ADEQUACY OF CONTROL WORKSHEET

The more difficult aspect of the control review is Step 3, involving determining the adequacy of control. **Figure 4-1, Determining the Adequacy of Control,** which was designed for this purpose, is completed as follows:

Concern: One sheet should be prepared for each concern identified on Figure 3-1.

No. (#):   The sequential number used to identify the concern on Figure 3-5.

Figure 4-1

DETERMINING THE ADEQUACY OF CONTROL

Concern: _____ # _____

Magnitude Of Concern: ☐ High

☐ Medium

☐ Low

Controls:

Checklist #
Reference _____ Description (Optional) _____

Strength Of Controls: ☐ High

☐ Medium

☐ Low

Adequacy Of Controls: ☐ More Than Adequate

☐ Adequate

☐ Less Than Adequate

Magnitude of Concern:	The reviewer should make a determination as to whether the concern is of high, medium, or low magnitude. The concern will be relative to the size and assets controlled by the organization. Normally, these are more relative terms, meaning the relationship of one concern to another, as opposed to the actual dollar amount of the concern.
Controls:	This part of the worksheet should identify all of the controls that are believed helpful in reducing the threat of loss due to the concern. These controls can be identified by either using the checklists provided in a later part of this section, or through inquiry or investigation (note that organizations may have controls which are not identified on the latter checklists). If the controls are on the checklist, the checklist number and item number can be used to identify the control, with the description of the control being optional. If the control is not on the checklist, then it should be described.
Strength of Controls:	The reviewer must make an assessment as to whether the strength of the controls is high, medium, or low. High-strength controls are those in which the organization should be able to place great reliance, medium-strength controls are those on which the organization can place reliance, and low-strength controls are those controls on which the organization can only place minor reliance. In other words, the controls of lower- or medium-strength may not be effective in all situations.
Adequacy of Controls:	To determine the adequacy, the reviewer would compare the magnitude of the concern to the strength of the control. If they are equal, in other words the concern is high and the strength of the control is high, then the controls should be checked as adequate. If the strength of the controls is greater than the magnitude of the concern (for example, the strength of the controls is high while the magnitude of the concern is medium) then the control should be considered more than adequate. On the other hand, if the magnitude of the concern is greater than the strength of the controls, then the adequacy should be stated as less than adequate.

4.2   HOW TO USE CONTROL CHECKLISTS

The checklists are designed primarily to identify controls for the assessment process. Prior to using the checklists, the review team should:

1.   Read through the checklist in detail.

57

2. Ensure that the reviewer using the checklist understands each of the items (e.g., control questions). If the reviewer does not understand the question, he or she should ask other members of the review team their interpretation of the item, or that item should be deleted from the review process.

3. Delete any questions that are not applicable to the concerns being reviewed.

4. Add any questions that in the reviewer's knowledge would identify controls not included on the checklist.

It is also advisable, but not essential, to ensure that it is within the reviewer's prerogative to ask the questions included on the checklist. Note that in some instances organizations' policies, procedure, or line of business may exclude that area from the prerogative of the review. For example, fire may be a corporate disaster problem, as opposed to a computer system disaster problem. In that case, the review program itself would not include items related to fire, and thus the review process should not be asking those questions.

The checklist can be used in any of the following three manners:

1. **Given to computer operations to answer:**

   The questions can be handed to computer operations for them to answer at their leisure. Once computer operations has provided the answer, the review team can review the answers and do any additional probing they believe necessary.

2. **Ask the appropriate individual the question:**

   The review team can ask the computer operations or other involved personnel the questions one by one. The reviewer can then record the answer on the checklist and make any notations or qualifications that are appropriate.

3. **Do probing and answer the questions later:**

   The reviewer can hold general interviews and discussions with a variety of people involved in the disaster recovery process. This probing is general in nature, although based on the questions included within the checklist. After the reviewer has finished the probing interview/investigations, the reviewer then asks himself/herself the questions and responds to them based on the information gathered during the investigation. If the reviewer is unable to answer the question, additional investigation may have to be undertaken.

4.3   DISASTER RECOVERY CONTROL CHECKLISTS

The following six disaster recovery control checklists are provided to review the adequacy of disaster recovery controls:

(Note that these questions are applicable to all of the above given checklists)

Each checklist is divided into the following three sections:

1.   Items related to the financial loss objective of disaster recovery

2.   Items related to the legal responsibility aspect of disaster recovery

3.   Items related to the business service interruption aspects of disaster recovery

The reviewer using the checklist should go to those parts of the checklist that relate to the objective impacted which was checked for each of the disaster recovery concerns in Figure 3-5. This should prove helpful in selecting the appropriate questions for the conduct of static tests to evaluate whether the controls have adequately addressed the concern.

Figure 4-2

VITAL RECORDS DISASTER RECOVERY CONTROL CHECKLIST

No.	Item	Responses			Comments
		Yes	No	N/A	
	BUSINESS SERVICE INTERRUPTION				
1.	Have the vital documents and records of the organization been thoroughly analyzed and control procedures set up?				
2.	Does the organization use a remote, safe document storage vault?				
3.	Are copies of all valuable documents stored in a remote safe storage vault?				
4.	Are applications and operations documentation of programs handling vital information backed up in safe storage?				
5.	Is there a document that specifies what information must be retained, and for how long?				
	FINANCIAL LOSS				
1.	Do safes and vaults carry the Safe Manufacturers National Association or the Underwriters Laboratories seal?				
2.	Does your organization maintain an inventory of vital records for insurance purposes?				
3.	Are your tapes and disks stored away from outside walls so as not to be damaged in the event of bombing?				
	LEGAL RESPONSIBILITY				
1.	Is the legal department satisfied with the EDP handling of vital documents?				
2.	Have the retention periods of all data processing files and documents been reviewed to ensure they are in compliance with legal requirements?				
3.	Is your record retention in compliance with your insurance requirements?				
4.	Do you use a paper shredder or an incinerator to destroy important documents?				

Figure 4-3
(Page 1)

APPLICATION SYSTEMS DISASTER RECOVERY CONTROL CHECKLIST

No.	Item	Responses			Comments
		Yes	No	N/A	
	BUSINESS SERVICE INTERRUPTION				
1.	For on-line customer services, can alternate operations be brought up within the predefined time frame?				
2.	Are systems analysts instructed to incorporate disaster recovery requirements into application requirements?				
3.	Are source documents stored by the control function after data entry?				
4.	Has protection been standardized to protect critical files against programming errors, operator errors, and system errors?				
5.	Are new versions of computer programs backed up within a reasonable period after those versions are put into production?				
6.	Are all program changes made at the source level, then recompiled and tested?				
7.	Is there audit trail information produced in all financial systems?				
8.	Are there programs available that will handle teleprocessing jobs in the batch mode at the terminal site or at the central site?				
9.	If there are backup programs to perform teleprocessing work in the batch mode, have they been tested?				
10.	Have alternate processing procedures taken into account the data preparation and key entry process?				
11.	Is test data maintained for each application system so that in the event of a disaster the application can be tested to ensure that it functions properly?				

Figure 4-3
(Page 2)

APPLICATION SYSTEMS DISASTER RECOVERY CONTROL CHECKLIST

No.	Item	Responses			Comments
		Yes	No	N/A	
	BUSINESS SERVICE INTERRUPTION (Cont.)				
12.	Are backup copies of the application source codes maintained in an off-site storage facility?				
13.	If you have purchased applications, can the vendors supply extra copies of those applications in the event of an emergency?				
14.	Is your documentation prepared using a typewriter or pen ink which is water insoluble, so that it still is readable if exposed to water?				
15.	In the event that preprinted forms are unavailable, could the applications be processed using application-created headings and forms?				
16.	Are your applications classified to continue processing in the event of a mail stoppage?				
17.	Does your application processing documentation call for an orderly shutdown of applications in the event of a disaster?				
18.	Has a priority listing been established for all of the terminal site work priorities?				
	FINANCIAL LOSS				
1.	Has management strictly prioritized the most necessary services to be maintained in an emergency?				
2.	Did all user groups involved in customer services and cash handling participate in the development of the disaster recovery procedures?				
3.	Are most cash deposits handled so as not to be vulnerable to a disaster in the computer area?				

Figure 4-3
(Page 3)

APPLICATION SYSTEMS DISASTER RECOVERY CONTROL CHECKLIST

No.	Item	Responses			Comments
		Yes	No	N/A	
	FINANCIAL LOSS (Cont.)				
4.	Does the organization have plans for controlled public press releases in times of disaster?				
5.	Are all program changes approved and signed off by user personnel?				
6.	Is there routine logging of all communication transactions in a form that can be rapidly traced?				
7.	Are there checkpoints in large programs so that they can be restarted at other than the beginning of program processing?				
8.	If alternate site processing is used in the event of a disaster, have arrangements been made to transport data to and from the alternate site?				
9.	Have the financial risks associated with computer disaster been estimated?				
10.	Has a cost/benefit study been made on the disaster recovery plan?				
11.	Has the financial loss associated with each type of disaster been estimated?				
12.	Does insurance cover any monetary loss resulting from total or partial loss of business due to the inability of the computer center to operate?				
13.	Does your disaster plan include notifying customers of delays or other problems in the event of a computer disaster?				
14.	Have you made arrangements with your key customers to satisfy their emergency requirements in the event that periods of computer downtime prevent your normal interaction with them?				

Figure 4-3
(Page 4)

APPLICATION SYSTEMS DISASTER RECOVERY CONTROL CHECKLIST

No.	Item	Responses			Comments
		Yes	No	N/A	
	LEGAL RESPONSIBILITY				
1.	Have the system designers and/or users designated the files that are critical to the organization, and are those files appropriately backed up?				
2.	Are purchased applications protected in accordance with the contractual legal requirements during periods of disaster?				
3.	Is an adequate audit trail created and protected in accordance with Internal Revenue Service requirements for all financial applications?				

Figure 4-4
(Page 1)

HARDWARE/SOFTWARE DISASTER RECOVERY CONTROL CHECKLIST

No.	Item	Responses			Comments
		Yes	No	N/A	
	BUSINESS SERVICE INTERRUPTION				
1.	Have discussions been held with all equipment vendors as to their response to an emergency situation?				
2.	Are smoke and fire detectors installed throughout the computer area?				
3.	Are there written backup procedures for all terminal sites?				
4.	Are the backup procedures periodically tested at terminal sites?				
5.	In the case of a disaster affecting communication lines, is it possible to transmit the high-priority terminal work via Western Union, TWX, or Bell Telephone?				
6.	In the event of a communications disaster, is it possible to transmit priority work via vehicle pickup and delivery?				
7.	Have alternate sites been selected for processing in the event a primary source of power is lost?				
8.	Have alternative sources of power been arranged for in the event that the primary source of power is lost?				
9.	Are noncompany backup sites regularly contacted to ensure that they will have adequate time for processing in the event of a computer disaster in your organization?				
10.	Do you regularly check with backup sites to ensure that their hardware is still compatible with the hardware needed for backup purposes?				
11.	Are the operating system and other operating software packages backed up in off-site storage areas?				

Figure 4-4
(Page 2)

HARDWARE/SOFTWARE DISASTER RECOVERY CONTROL CHECKLIST

No.	Item	Responses			Comments
		Yes	No	N/A	
	BUSINESS SERVICE INTERRUPTION (Cont.)				
12.	Is the backup version of operating software up to date?				
13.	Have you tested your operating software in the backup hardware site(s)?				
14.	Do you maintain supplies of critical hardware items, such as cable and extra terminals, in the event that the primary hardware becomes defective?				
15.	Can your hardware vendors supply extra hardware during an emergency?				
16.	Can your software vendors supply extra copies of software in the event of emergency?				
17	Have you made arrangements with your hardware vendor to get emergency maintenance service during nonworking hours in the event of a disaster?				
18.	If your hardware is water cooled, have you made arrangements for alternate water supplies in the event that your primary source is interrupted?				
19.	Does your emergency plan call for the orderly shutdown of processing in the event of a disaster?				
	FINANCIAL LOSS				
1.	Is all computer hardware protected by fire protection equipment?				
2.	Has a test of fire detection and extinguishing equipment been held in the past six months?				
3.	Is a central Halon system or equivalent used to protect the computer facility?				

Figure 4-4
(Page 3)

HARDWARE/SOFTWARE DISASTER RECOVERY CONTROL CHECKLIST

No.	Item	Responses			Comments
		Yes	No	N/A	
	FINANCIAL LOSS (Cont.)				
4.	Is there a fire alarm system connected to the computer room air conditioning system that sounds when the air conditioning is turned off?				
5.	Is there an audible or visible alarm when temperature and humidity limits are exceeded?				
6.	If the alternate site is under the operation of another organization, has an agreement been signed with that organization for backup purposes?				
7.	Does your organization maintain an inventory of hardware and software for insurance purposes?				
8.	Are waterproof covers available to cover the hardware in the event of water leakage from floors above the computer center?				
9.	Have acceptable downtime tolerances been established for each piece of hardware, and if the hardware exceeds that, are the vendors contacted to remedy the situation?				
	LEGAL RESPONSIBILITY				
1.	If the equipment is leased, is it adequately protected in the event of a disaster, according to the lease?				

Figure 4-5
(Page 1)

PERSONNEL DISASTER RECOVERY CONTROL CHECKLIST

No.	Item	Responses			Comments
		Yes	No	N/A	
	BUSINESS SERVICE INTERRUPTION				
1.	Do all staff members know who to call in times of emergency or where the emergency telephone list is located?				
2.	Have operating personnel been trained in fire reporting and fire fighting procedures?				
3.	Have attempts been made to create and sustain employee interest in the prevention of fire, theft, and other causes of disaster?				
4.	Have alternates been assigned to all disaster recovery jobs in case of absence of the primary handler?				
5.	Are assignment records kept up-to-date?				
6.	Have employees been educated in the importance of disaster recovery procedures?				
7.	Are lists of all vendors maintained in a disaster recovery documentation?				
8.	Are operator manuals backed up off-site?				
9.	Are operator instructions clear and complete?				
10.	Is there a permanent disaster recovery planning team or equivalent?				
11.	Has an emergency organizational chart been developed?				
12.	Have employee call-in lists been prepared for use during a disaster?				
13.	Are there general community procedures designed to notify the entire work force, over radio or TV, in the event of a serious disaster?				
14.	Are management personnel able to run the computer center in the event nonmanagement personnel are unavailable?				

Figure 4-5
(Page 2)

PERSONNEL DISASTER RECOVERY CONTROL CHECKLIST

No.	Item	Responses			Comments
		Yes	No	N/A	
	BUSINESS SERVICE INTERRUPTION (Cont.)				
15.	Has a personal skills inventory been conducted to identify special employee skills that could be used during an emergency (e.g., volunteer fireman, etc.)?				
16.	Is the traffic flow of non-DP employees routed away from the computer center facilities?				
	FINANCIAL LOSS				
1.	Are entrances to the data processing areas supervised?				
2.	Do personnel who have been terminated with cause leave immediately?				
3.	Is access to the data library restricted to designated librarians, even during disaster periods?				
4.	Has a recovery team been assigned so that they can begin work immediately in the event of a disaster?				
5.	Is user management heavily involved in computer disaster recovery planning?				
6.	Are computer personnel in key positions of authority bonded?				
7.	Are key personnel continually reviewed for their potential as a threat to the organization?				
8.	Are key personnel subject to background checks before they are hired or moved into key positions?				
9.	Are computer operations personnel prohibited from eating, smoking, or doing other activities in the computer room which might be detrimental to the computer hardware and applications?				

Figure 4-5
(Page 3)

PERSONNEL DISASTER RECOVERY CONTROL CHECKLIST

No.	Item	Responses			Comments
		Yes	No	N/A	
	LEGAL RESPONSIBILITY				
1.	Has the staff been trained in fire alarm, bomb threat, and other emergency procedures?				
2.	Has the staff been adequately instructed in what to do when an emergency alarm sounds?				
3.	Are personnel given a debriefing before they terminate or transfer to other areas of the organization?				
4.	Is an employee's ID badge collected before he/she leaves the company?				
5.	Have computer center personnel been trained concerning the protection of confidential data during periods of disaster recovery?				
6.	Are unexplained gaps in the recorded meter readings checked?				
7.	Do all security procedures remain in effect during a disaster recovery period?				
8.	Have individuals been assigned to specific areas for evacuation of the building, and have those individuals been trained in their jobs?				
9.	Have communication procedures been established to inform all personnel of emergency situations?				
10.	Have arrangements been made to handle visitors during an emergency situation?				
11.	Are new or transferred employees immediately trained in disaster recovery procedures and assigned appropriate responsibilities?				
12.	Are disaster recovery responsibilities included in the appropriate individuals' job description?				

Figure 4-5
(Page 4)

PERSONNEL DISASTER RECOVERY CONTROL CHECKLIST

No.	Item	Responses			Comments
		Yes	No	N/A	
	LEGAL RESPONSIBILITY (Cont.)				
13.	Does your insurance cover personal injuries to help protect against libel, defamation of character, or invasion of privacy suits?				
14.	Are key employees asked to sign statements that they understand the policies and procedures of data processing and will abide by and enforce those procedures?				

Figure 4-6
(Page 1)

SUPPLIES/FACILITIES DISASTER RECOVERY CONTROL CHECKLIST

No.	Item	Responses			Comments
		Yes	No	N/A	
	BUSINESS SERVICE INTERRUPTION				
1.	Is there a complete listing of all supplies and copies of all forms available in a second site?				
2.	Are emergency backups of critical forms held in a second site?				
3.	Will emergency processing sites have access to the normal support supplies such as a personnel telephone directory, company stationery, etc.?				
4.	Do backup personnel have keys or other access to the facility in the event of an emerge4.Do backup personnel have keys or other access to the facility in the event of an emergency when the facility was locked?				
5.	Are architectural drawings of the electricity, water, etc. maintained in an off-site location for use in the event of a disaster?				
6.	Have you made arrangements with your vendors for alternate delivery or quantity of supplies in the event of a disaster?				
7.	Have you made arrangements with your vendors to acquire extra supplies during vendor non-working hours in the event of a disaster?				
	FINANCIAL LOSS				
1.	Are all working and storage areas for data processing documents protected by sprinkler systems?				
2.	Are there formal emergency procedures that cover the handling of all the major emergency situations?				
3.	Has the local fire department been called in to provide advice and to familiarize themselves with the computer center and its unique problems?				

Figure 4-6
(Page 2)

SUPPLIES/FACILITIES DISASTER RECOVERY CONTROL CHECKLIST

No.	Item	Responses			Comments
		Yes	No	N/A	
	FINANCIAL LOSS (Cont.)				
4.	Is a fire survey made regularly by either insurance or fire department personnel?				
5.	Have the operating personnel been assigned individual responsibilities in case of fire?				
6	Have all floors, including floors above and floors below, in multiple tenant buildings been checked to ensure adequate fireproofing, waterproofing, and noncollapsible support?				
7.	Are all exterior doors of sufficient strength to deter impluse intrusion (i.e., pushing)?				
8.	Have high-pressure steam lines and water lines been routed away from the computer room?				
9.	Is the computer site away from natural disaster areas, such as flood plains?				
10.	Does insurance cover data processing media, such as magnetic disks, printed forms, etc.?				
11.	Does insurance cover the computer site furnishings, such as data storage cabinets and racks?				
12.	Does your organization maintain an inventory of supplies and other assets located at your computer facility for insurance purposes?				
13.	Are fire extinguishers and other emergency equipment located in convenient locations in the computer site?				
14.	Are air filters, acoustical tiles, and other materials inside the data processing equipment made of noncombustible material?				

Figure 4-6
(Page 3)

SUPPLIES/FACILITIES DISASTER RECOVERY CONTROL CHECKLIST

No.	Item	Responses			Comments
		Yes	No	N/A	
	LEGAL RESPONSIBILITY				
1.	Are the organization's fire, safety, and engineering people working closely with the team establishing the disaster recovery programs?				
2.	Have the fire and safety systems in the EDP facility area been reviewed by an independent person?				
3.	Are safes and vaults provided for all important documents and files?				
4.	Is there a controlled access system of admittance to the computer area by positive identification?				

Figure 4-7
(Page 1)

GENERAL DISASTER RECOVERY CONTROL CHECKLIST

No.	Item	Responses			Comments
		Yes	No	N/A	
	BUSINESS SERVICE INTERRUPTION				
1.	Has the disaster recovery plan been reviewed by senior management and approved by all responsible managers?				
2.	Are the procedures clear and simple enough for use during an emergency?				
3.	Is the plan orderly and up to date?				
4.	Are the procedures and responsibilities defined clearly by individual or position?				
5.	Is the disaster recovery plan tested at least annually?				
6.	Have management notification procedures been developed for any emergency of any size?				
7.	Have specific personnel been assigned the responsibility for supervising the performance of emergency procedures?				
8.	Have the individual types of disaster been identified?				
9.	Has the full disaster plan been documented?				
10.	Is the formal disaster recovery plan regularly updated as processing conditions and personnel change?				
11.	Are changes to the disaster recovery plan tested, or evaluated by an independent group?				
12.	Have you invited the following public and utility services to tour your premises to advise you on possible danger areas: electric utility, fire department, police department, water department, and gas utility?				
13.	Are extra copies of the disaster recovery plans maintained in secure locations?				
14.	If extra copies of the disaster recovery plan are maintained, are they regularly updated?				

Figure 4-7
(Page 2)

GENERAL DISASTER RECOVERY CONTROL CHECKLIST

No.	Item	Responses			Comments
		Yes	No	N/A	
	FINANCIAL LOSS				
1.	Is the disaster recovery plan tailored to the organization?				
2.	Is the plan well documented and understood?				
3.	Are there written procedures which explain the organization's security system and define the responsibilities of the personnel for security?				
4.	Has the possibility of insurance been investigated and a decision made on the desirability of acquiring insurance against computer disasters?				
5.	Has a disaster recovery plan been developed for each type of significant disaster?				
6.	Is the insurance coverage for computer disasters regularly reviewed for adequacy?				
7.	In the event of a disaster, have sufficient funds been allocated for transportation, operating expenses, emergency supplies, etc.?				
8.	Does disaster insurance cover extra expenses (defined as the excess of the total cost during the period of restoration of the operation of the business over and above the total cost of such operation that would normally have occurred during the same period had no loss occurred)?				
9.	Is your insurance coverage up to date with respect to the current assets owned by the organization?				
	LEGAL RESPONSIBILITY				
1.	Has the disaster recovery plan been reviewed by legal counsel to ensure that it is reasonable based on the provisions of the Foreign Corrupt Practices Act of 1977?				

Figure 4-7
(Page 3)

GENERAL DISASTER RECOVERY CONTROL CHECKLIST

No.	Item	Responses			Comments
		Yes	No	N/A	
	LEGAL RESPONSIBILITY (Cont.)				
2.	Does the plan adequately protect the privacy of information about individuals?				
3.	Do the disaster recovery planning teams understand that the protection and safety of people in the area is paramount?				
4.	Does management enforce security procedures, and punish violators?				
5.	Do the auditors review disaster recovery programs to ensure they are in conformance with legal requirements?				

SECTION 5

TESTING THE DISASTER RECOVERY PROGRAM

SECTION OVERVIEW

Testing is the verification that part or all of the disaster recovery program performs as stated. Testing can be as simple as examining the existence of documentation, or as complex as simulating disasters. This section explains the objectives of disaster recovery testing, and some of the more common methods of conducting those tests. Lastly, the section provides a decision table as a tool in helping to select the appropriate testing technique, and in the evaluation of the results of a disaster recovery test.

5.1   OBJECTIVES OF TESTING DISASTER RECOVERY PROCEDURES

Experts in disaster recovery state that breakdowns almost always occur at the weakest link. The disaster recovery process must be considered a chain comprised of many links. Each link is a safeguard. In other words, disaster recovery fails because some condition, often minor, has been overlooked.

What this means in testing disaster recovery is that the emphasis should be placed on looking for the weakest link. Personnel not trained in disaster recovery cannot hope to evaluate the effectiveness of sophisticated measures, nor design safeguards against complex problems. What they can logically hope to do is find the weaker links and shore up the safeguards in that area.

The disaster recovery testing procedures discussed in this section are not sophisticated. They are not designed to assess the adequacy of the procedures against major disasters. As previously stated, they are designed to uncover weak links. Once uncovered, additional measures can be installed to improve overall disaster recovery procedures.

The objectives of conducting disaster recovery tests by nonprofessionals are:

- To provide an assessment of disaster recovery procedures in order to pinpoint the weaker areas.

- To conduct tests to determine whether the installed disaster recovery procedures are operational.

- To conduct tests to ensure whether the installed disaster recovery procedures are effective.

- To create an awareness on the part of employees that management is truly concerned with disaster recovery procedures (i.e., concerned enough to test them).

- To help educate management as to the degree of disaster recovery procedures installed, and what measures could be added to increase disaster recovery procedures.

5.2   APPROACHES FOR TESTING DISASTER RECOVERY PROCEDURES

The disaster recovery procedures covered in this section can be conducted by anyone with a general familiarity with data processing. It is not necessary to have a background in disaster recovery procedures and investigation, although it would be helpful. The individual utilizing these approaches should have some background in the following areas:

- **Data processing concepts:**   A general understanding of how systems are built and operated on data processing equipment.

- **Understanding of computer operating concepts:** A general understanding of the flow of work in and out of the computer room, including the data library and backup facilities.

- **General knowledge of the business:** An understanding of the lines of business in which the organization is engaged, and how data processing fits into the day-to-day operation of those lines of business.

- **Management philosophy:** An understanding of management's disaster recovery procedure objectives, and the means and severity of its disaster recovery procedure concerns.

- **Auditing concepts:** A general understanding of how to conduct a review, and write a report based on that review.

It is not necessary for an individual to have an in-depth background in any of these areas, but the individual should have an overall understanding of each area. With this background, the individual may begin testing disaster recovery procedures.

5.2.1   CATEGORIES OF TESTING

There are three areas in which disaster recovery procedures can be tested. These areas are:

- **Static testing of disaster recovery logical procedures:** This approach begins with the assumption that there are disaster recovery exposures general to all organizations. Once these exposures are identified, tests can be conducted to determine whether or not adequate procedures are in place to lessen the exposures. These tests primarily involve conducting exposure scenarios.

- **Dynamically testing disaster recovery logical procedures:** There are two general types of disaster recovery. One is physical and one is logical. Programs are the means of enforcing logical disaster recovery. Programs can enforce disaster recovery through both the application system and the operating system. It is through the use of program logic that problems can be prevented, detected, and the necessary information made available to correct problems once they are detected. Programs can be evaluated in both a static and dynamic environment. These tests do a dynamic analysis.

- **Testing physical disaster recovery (using audit techniques):** Auditors have been testing the adequacy of disaster recovery for a number of years. In this process, they have perfected several techniques which have proven effective in assessing disaster recovery. Those wishing to evaluate the effectiveness of physical disaster recovery can use the same techniques.

Prior to testing disaster recovery, the objectives of the test should be clearly established. The objectives should be the concerns defined in Figure 3-5. Once these objectives are known, the appropriate testing approach can be selected. The last part of this section is a worksheet designed to aid in selecting the appropriate testing technique.

We will discuss each of these approaches, and the techniques available for each approach. From studying the techniques, one can determine in which instances those techniques are most effective in testing security.

5.3   STATIC TESTING OF DISASTER RECOVERY LOGICAL PROCEDURES

Static disaster recovery must:

1.   Provide evidence that the disaster recovery procedure satisfies its mission, requirements, and specifications.

2.   Evaluate disaster recovery mechanisms to maintain adequate levels of performance in the face of unexpected behavior in the environment, as can occur from acts of nature, procedural program flaws, operator goofs, etc.

Combinations of the following examination approaches are currently being used by industry:

- **Design Review:**

   This method entails a formal meeting of the designers with reviewers to scrutinize the disaster recovery design against mission and requirements. The product design should include narrative documents, logic diagrams, and functional specification. It may include results of tests for critical components. Design reviews should be scheduled milestones for each subsystem and major components. Results must be documented and communicated to all participants.

- **Peer Review:**

   The classical scientific method is to invite professional peer review and comment on the product at various stages of development and change. This tends to be a less structured review, as it relies on the experiences of the peers.

- **Quality Control (QC):**

   A third part (neither customer nor developer) is committed to check the quality of all disaster recovery procedures. This technique combines 1 and 2 above in a formal, often contractual manner. The OC contractor is selected because of its experience, tools, personnel, and skill in such work.

- ### Software Checking:

  This technique evaluates applications to determine that they provide an adequate audit trail for recovery. Source-code-to-object-code translators (i.e., compilers) have always been used to detect program errors as a QC tool. New languages demand explicit, detailed declarations of a programmer's intent with strong data typing, restricted program scopes, rigid module calling sequences, etc., that force structured programming. The compilers for these languages do extensive and complete checking to enforce the language syntax and semantics, and in some cases generate code for run-time enforcement of program assertions.

- ### Automated Analyzers:

  This technique also evaluates application recovery procedures. A number of source-code tools are available that perform some of the syntax and semantic analysis of a compiler, but do not generate object code. Such tools are used to produce flow diagrams, reformat code to aid documentation, produce cross-reference listings and indices for improved library control and use, and to produce test cases for dynamic evaluation. Newer uses are to automatically generate truth assertions about the program to assist in the formal proof of correctness.

- ### Formal Proof:

  Formal proof of program correctness is the leading edge of the state-of-the-art. Basically, the method accepts "correctness criteria" and the "program" as input and produces as output a formal proof (or counter-example) that the program satisfies the correctness criteria. In practice, the technique is iterative for each part of the disaster recovery program stage. At the top level, the correctness criteria are a set of truth assertions and mathematical models of program requirements. The program is a mathematical specification. Both are expressed in a "specification language." At each level, these inputs - criteria and program - are processed through a "Verification Condition Generator", which produces a set of conditions to be verified. The "verification conditions", e.g., source program and truth assertions, are processed by a "Theorem Prover" producing a formal mathematical proof of correctness - i.e., a proof that the source program satisfies the truth assertions. The process can be manual or automated. A number of quite restricted "programs" have been proved both manually and with automated aids.

5.4   DYNAMICALLY TESTING DISASTER RECOVERY LOGICAL PROCEDURES

Essentially, this approach "runs the program and sees if it works." Unlike static evaluation, dynamic evaluation also tests for errors introduced by the compiler, loader, operating system, libraries and support packages, physical procedures, communication elements, and CPU hardware. Static evaluation tries to exhaust all program conditions; dynamic execution involves real time and is practical only for selected test cases. Therein lies the basic "art" of testing, that is, choosing the best test cases. Many schemes exist. Department of Defense (DOD) testing requires three stages: (1) unit testing of discrete modules; (2) subsystems testing of the integrated collection of modules; and (3) system testing of the integrated collection of subsystems, actual hardware, and real data. This is a reasonable paradigm for other approaches.

Testing should not end after system delivery, but be continuous. A number of schemes have been successful.

- **Exercising:**

  The system is tested by running simulated operations with known responses that are compared against test results. This is a well known approach in testing DOD systems in the field. A modified version has seen recent application in the commercial sector, where a simulated minicompany is established in a corporation's financial control system so that the auditor can easily observe the system's response to test input to the minicompany. The minicompany approach is also known as the Integrated Test Facility (ITF) method.

- **Flaw Hypothesis Method:**

  In this approach, system flaws are hypothesized based on analogous flaws found in other systems, and are tested for existence on the object system. It is a cost-effective approach to test case selection.

- **Surprise Test:**

  Based on the military's Inspector General scheme, the test team arrives unannounced and runs tests on the live system. Such schemes exercise the current live system and uncover possible unauthorized versions or modified operating procedures.

- **Reasonableness Checks:**

  The system is tested on its ability to detect and recover from typical human errors such as typographical errors, out-of-context actions, nonsense commands (e.g., rewind card reader), etc.

- **Error Recovery:**

  The system is tested on its ability to detect and recover from a variety of hardware, communications, power interruptions and surges, and program errors. Of particular interest is restart, check-point, and roll-back options.

- **On-Line Monitoring and Control:**

  The functioning parts of the recovery program can be observed by monitoring events as they occur. This can be performed in a number of ways. One way is to insert a routine in an operating system exit that logs the type of events that occur, which can then be checked against what should occur. In other instances, monitoring can be done from the operator terminal, or an on-line system from the master terminal. Some organizations have acquired hardware and software monitors which provide information on the functioning of the system. In some instances, those commercially available monitors can provide information on the adequacy of the information gathered for disaster recovery. In some instances where processing is switched between processors based on problems, that switching can also be monitored on-line.

5.5 TESTING PHYSICAL DISASTER RECOVERY PROCEDURES (USING AUDIT TECHNIQUES)

Individuals testing physical disaster recovery procedures can utilize the same techniques used by auditors. These techniques have been used successfully for years in probing the adequacy of disaster recovery procedure systems. Some only require minimal skills, but others require extensive data processing skills.

Three audit techniques are readily applicable to testing physical disaster recovery procedures. These are:

- Audit guides (requires data processing skills)

- Job accounting systems (requires extensive data processing skills)

- Disaster testing (requires minimal skills)

These techniques are discussed individually.

5.5.1 AUDIT GUIDES

An audit guide provides guidance to internal auditors on how to accomplish an audit of an area (e.g., computer service center) or a system (e.g., computer application system) by means of questions, follow up actions, and steps to perform. Audit guides for auditors have proved their value over years of usage. The use of audit guides in the computer area is a natural extension from the audit of manual systems. The prime difference between audit guides for manual systems and audit guides for computer systems is in the data processing background necessary to use the data processing auditing guide effectively. Without this data processing background, the auditor will be unable to comprehend the importance or meaning behind some of the questions in the guide.

Audit guides are used by internal auditors to evaluate performance with regard to use of resources (efficiency) as well as in terms of the satisfaction achieved by the users (effectiveness) of computer application systems. The use of audit guides reduces preparation time by taking advantage of past experience, and provides uniformity for the evaluation process.

Audit guides provide a step-by-step process that can be used to review security. The guide covers all aspects of the review and will lead the less experienced through a complex audit. The Auditing Computer Systems manual, a publication of the FTP Technical Library, is one of the better guides for auditors in the computer area.

The success of using an audit guide depends upon the thorough formulation of an approach or work plan. During the development of the work plan, it is important to keep in focus the objective and scope of the audit. With this in mind, the formulation of a work plan using an audit guide should include the following steps:

- Obtain an understanding of the organization's policies, procedures, and practices pertaining to the application system under review.

- Obtain a general understanding of the area under audit, including the intended purpose or function, the requirements of the user community, the source and flow of data, the processing requirements, and the relevant time constraints.

- Identify specific data processing steps, interfaces with other applications and outputs which are utilized throughout the application.

- Identify specific control features or points.

- Identify potential threats.

- Decide upon the methodology (i.e., audit tools and methods) that will be used when conducting the audit.

- Obtain an understanding of the human factors that affect the area, including the human engineering aspects of the user interface as well as personnel areas such as hiring and termination practices, employee morale, vacation and job rotation.

- Obtain an understanding of the hardware, software and systems technologies used.

- Obtain an understanding of the training and continuing education programs offered by the organization.

- Obtain an understanding of the system's development, implementation and maintenance controls.

- Decide on the form of reporting the findings, conclusions, and recommendations of the audit.

- Decide on review procedures for the audit that will assure high technical quality.

- Decide on audit staffing and project control methods.

Once the objective, scope, approach and work plan for the audit have been established, the audit should be conducted using appropriate audit tools and methods. Following the audit, a draft report of findings, conclusions, and recommendations should be prepared, reviewed with appropriate management personnel, and submitted in final form. If corrective measures have been recommended, the managers ultimately responsible should be required to respond, in writing, regarding planned actions.

5.5.2   JOB ACCOUNTING DATA ANALYSIS

Job account facilities are available through most computer vendors as an adjunct to their operating systems. The job accounting facility is a feature of the computer operating system software that provides the means for gathering and recording information used for billing customers for evaluating systems usage. Examples of information collected by a job accounting facility are job start and completion times, usage of data sets, and usage of hardware facilities. These job accounting systems were designed by the vendors to serve the operating needs of the data processing department. However, much of the information provided by these facilities is of interest to internal auditors.

Two types of job accounting data, the account records and the data set activity records, are of interest to the internal auditor. Accounting records consist of records that show which user used which programs, how often, and for how long. They include an identification of the user, the hardware features required by the job, the time it took to perform the job, and how the job was completed. Data set activity records provide information about which data files were used during processing and who requested the use of the data sets. Among the information contained in these records are the data set name, record length, serial number of the volumes, and the user of the data set.

The internal auditor can use data from the accounting records to verify charges for the use of the computer resources. They also enable the auditor to verify that only authorized individuals used the computer. Data set activity records provide the auditor with a means to verify that the data are being used by authorized individuals.

Job accounting data can be utilized for many aspects of disaster recovery auditing. The two most prominent are:

- **Analysis of Data and File Creation:**

    Job accounting systems log a message each time a file is created. This log will show whether or not all the needed recovery data was created.

- **Analysis of Access to Data Files:**

    Each time a data file is opened, the job accounting systems log a message of that event. The message contains the file that was opened, the date it was opened, as well as the program that opened the data file. Using this information, a report can be prepared by data file name which shows who (i.e., the program that accessed the file) utilized that file, the number of times that individual utilized the file, and the dates on which it was used. This information can be presented to the owner of the file for verification that each access was authorized and made by those individuals on those dates.

5.5.3   DISASTER TESTING

Most computer service centers develop plans for dealing with possible disasters. The disaster testing technique tests the validity of these plans by exercising the methods that would be used in such an event. The disasters provided for range from theft up to the complete destruction of the computer service center.

The objective of a disaster plan is to ensure effective protection against loss of corporate information. The auditor, on an unannounced basis, simulates a disaster in the computer service center to test the adequacy of the center's contingency plans. The test is performed periodically.

There are a number of methods used in conducting disaster tests. The most effective is the limited disaster test. In this approach, only one application system is involved. Thus, it limits the time and effort required to verify the effectiveness of the disaster procedures.

In the limited disaster test, a major application is selected for test purposes. This makes the impact of the test much more realistic and attention-getting to top management.

Once the application has been selected, a time for the test must be determined. Again, judgment should be used in picking a date and time when resources are available at the computer center. To pick one of the busier times for computer operations would unnecessarily disrupt the normal operations of the organization.

At the time of the test, the individual conducting it declares a disaster in the computer room. This is normally unannounced. However, the manager of data processing has usually been advised shortly ahead of time, in an effort to obtain the manager's support for the test procedures. In a limited test, it is not necessary to shut down the computer room operation.

The individual conducting the test gathers together all the information pertaining to the application being tested. This includes the following:

- All data files pertaining to the application

- All input transactions for the application

- All operating documentation for the application

- All job control language or other necessary computer instructions to run the application

- All programs, and changes to programs, that are part of the application

- All backup material relating to that application contained in the computer room

87

Many times these are not physically removed but, rather, labeled with a special color label so that the operators know they cannot be used during the test. When all information relating to the application being tested has been properly secured, data processing operations personnel are asked to rerun the most recent run. This will require them to have all the necessary backup.

Depending on the degree of test, computer operations may be asked to run the test on another computer. In that circumstance, they can be asked to do it without using any information within the computer center whose destruction was simulated.

At the completion of the disaster test, computer operations will know definitively whether or not their disaster plans work. Until a test of this type is conducted, there is the same uncertainty with a disaster plan as there is with other security safeguards. Until a safeguard is tested, one can never be sure whether it will function as designed.

5.6   SELECTING TESTING TECHNIQUES

Figure 5-1, Technique Selection, a decision table, follows to assist in selecting the appropriate test technique to meet your desired objective. This decision table can also be used as a brief summary of the available security testing techniques. You should begin at the first question and follow the path provided by your answers to questions until you reach an "END" statement. If your answer to a question is "no," go to the next question. This will either be at the appropriate technique to use, or it will state that no technique is available to meet your objective.

Figure 5-1
(Page 1)

TECHNIQUE SELECTION DECISION TABLE

Number	Question, or Technique to Use	If Yes, Go To Number	Comments
100	Do you want to review the disaster recovery controls?	200	
101	Do you want to test the disaster recovery logical procedures?	300	
102	Do you want to test the disaster recovery physical procedures?	400	
103	END		

Figure 5-1
(Page 2)

TECHNIQUE SELECTION DECISION TABLE

Number	Question, or Technique to Use	If Yes, Go To Number	Comments
200	Use the disaster recovery control checklists in Section 4		END

Figure 5-1
(Page 3)

TECHNIQUE SELECTION DECISION TABLE

Number	Question, or Technique to Use	If Yes, Go To Number	Comments
300	Do you want to test in a dynamic program environment?	350	
301	Do you want to test the application during the design phase?	311	
302	Do you want a peer group review of the security of the programs?	312	
303	Do you want the programs reviewed by an independent third party?	313	
304	Do you want source code compared to object code?	314	
305	Do you want to analyze the source code with an automated analyzer?	315	
306	Do you want a formal proof of program correctness?	316	
307	END		No Technique Available
311	Use the design review technique		END
312	Use the peer review technique		END
313	Use the quality control technique		END
314	Use the compiler checking technique		END
315	Use the automated analyzer technique		END
316	Use the formal proof technique		END

Figure 5-1
(Page 4)

TECHNIQUE SELECTION DECISION TABLE

Number	Question, or Technique to Use	If Yes, Go To Number	Comments
350	Do you want to run a simulated operation?	360	
351	Do you want to test for system flaws?	361	
352	Do you want a surprise test?	362	
353	Do you want to subject the system to reasonable human errors?	363	
354	Do you want to test the error recovery procedures?	364	
355	END		No Technique Available
360	Use the exercising technique		END
361	Use the flaw hypothesis method		END
362	Use the surprise test technique		END
363	Use the reasonableness check technique		END
364	Use the error recovery technique		END

Figure 5-1
(Page 5)

TECHNIQUE SELECTION DECISION TABLE

Number	Question, or Technique to Use	If Yes, Go To Number	Comments
400	Do you want to simulate a disaster in the computer room?	410	
401	Do you want to conduct a general review of physical security?	411	
402	Do you want to use the data collected during the computer operations for review purposes?	412	
403	END		No Technique Available
410	Use the disaster testing technique		END
411	Use the audit guide technique		END
412	Use the job accounting systems technique		END

5.7   EVALUATING THE RESULTS OF A DISASTER RECOVERY TEST

The evaluation of a disaster recovery test will be performed in one of the following two manners:

- **Static test:**   Judgment regarding the completeness of the material/procedure/process to perform a stated disaster recovery procedure.

- **Dynamic test:**   Evaluation of the results of the actual performance of a disaster recovery event versus the expected result of the disaster recovery test.

Evaluating tests is a more factual process than that of evaluating controls through control evaluation checklists. When tests are performed, the expected results of the test are measured against the actual results. The judgmental part is determining how adequate the actual results were in accomplishing the expected results.

The testing of a disaster recovery process involves the three evaluation steps after the test technique has been selected and the method of using that technique determined:

- **Step 1 - Determine Expected Results:**

    The individual conducting the test must determine prior to conducting the test what the expected results should be. Even if the individual is examining documentation, the individual should have predetermined the type and extent of documentation expected before the test occurs.

- **Step 2 - Execute Test and Produce Actual Results:**

    As a result of running the test, actual results should be produced. Again, even in a static test the actual results are what is found as a result of examining the documentation or other evidence.

- **Step 3 - Compare Actual to Expected Results:**

    At the conclusion of the test the actual and expected results should be compared. If there are no differences the procedure being tested can be considered adequate. If the results were less than expected, then the opinion based on the test would be less than adequate disaster recovery procedures. On the other hand, if the results far exceeded the expectations - if, for example, recovery was to occur within one hour and it actually occurred within fifteen minutes, then the results would be considered more than adequate.

Figure 5-2, Testing the Adequacy of Disaster Recovery Procedures, is provided as a tool for documenting the results of a test of a disaster recovery procedure. The form provides space to describe and document the test as well as develop an opinion on the adequacy of the disaster recovery procedure being tested. This worksheet will be used in developing the final evaluation of the adequacy of disaster recovery in the organization.

Figure 5-2

TESTING THE ADEQUACY OF DISASTER RECOVERY PROCEDURES

CONCERN: _____ # _____

DISASTER RECOVERY PROCEDURE(S) INVOLVED: _____

MAGNITUDE OF CONCERN: ☐ High

☐ Medium

☐ Low

ANALYSIS OF TESTS

Description Of Test(s)	Expected Results	Actual Results	Assessment of Test		
			More	Adeq.	Less

Result of Test

☐ High (Performance of Procedures)

☐ Medium (Performance of Procedures)

☐ Low (Performance of Procedures)

Adequacy of Disaster Recovery Procedure

☐ More Than Adequate

☐ Adequate

☐ Less Than Adequate

Figure 5-2 is completed as follows:

Concerns: One sheet should be prepared for each concern identified on Figure 3-5.

No. (#): The sequential number used to identify the concern on Figure 3-5.

Disaster Recovery Procedure(s) Involved: The organization will have developed one or more disaster recovery procedures to deal with each concern. Obviously, if there are no procedures, there can be no test. The individual conducting the test must identify which procedures, if they work, can reduce the identified concern.

Magnitude of Concern: The reviewer should make a determination as to whether the concern is of high, medium, or low magnitude to the organization. The concern will be relative to the size and assets controlled by the organization. Normally, these are relative terms, meaning the relationship of one concern to another, as opposed to the actual dollar amount of the concern.

Analysis of Tests: For each of the tests to be undertaken, the following information should be gathered:

- **Description of test(s):** The review team should describe the type of test it intends to conduct (note that this can be selected from the technique selection decision table in this chapter).

- **Expected results:** The result that the review team is expecting as a result of conducting the test (if more space is needed, additional sheets can be attached).

- **Actual results:** The actual results that occurred as a result of conducting the test (if more space is needed, additional sheets can be attached).

- **Assessment of test:** Based on the difference between the expected and actual results, in accordance with the above discussion, the assessment for each test should be one of the following:
  - More than adequate (More)
  - Adequate (Adeq.)
  - Less than adequate (Less)

Result of Test:

The reviewer must make an assessment as to whether the result of the test is high, medium, or low. High-result controls are those on which the organization should be able to place great reliance, medium-strength results are those on which the organization can place reliance, and low-strength results are those results on which the organization can only place minor reliance. In other words, the results of lower or medium strength may not be effective in all situations.

Adequacy of Disaster Recovery Procedure:

To determine the adequacy, the reviewer would compare the magnitude of the concern versus the strength of the results. If they are equal, in other words, if the concern is high and the strength of the results is high, then the disaster recovery procedure should be checked as adequate. If the strength of the results is greater than the magnitude of the concern (for example, if the strength of the result of tests is high while the magnitude of the concern is medium) then the adequacy of disaster recovery procedures should be considered as more than adequate. On the other hand, if the magnitude of the concern is greater than the result of test, then the procedure is less than adequate.

PART III

EVALUATING THE DISASTER RECOVERY PROGRAM

(Sections 6 and 7)

The final part of the review is to develop an opinion on the adequacy of the disaster recovery procedures. This part describes how to use the information gathered in Parts I and II of this manual in developing such an opinion.

SECTION 6

EVALUATING THE EFFECTIVENESS OF THE DISASTER RECOVERY PROGRAM

SECTION OVERVIEW

An opinion regarding the adequacy of the disaster recovery program is a judgment by the review team. However, this judgment should be supported by sufficient evidence collected during the review process. This section presents a method for organizing the review process and evaluation (as outlined in Sections 3-5) so as to develop an opinion. Each concern should be evaluated individually, and then the totality of the individual evaluations should be reviewed in making a final judgment on the adequacy of the disaster recovery program. The section also recommends the format of a report to management on the results of a disaster recovery review.

6.1 DEVELOPING A DISASTER RECOVERY OPINION

The review team can issue either or both of the following two opinions about the adequacy of the disaster recovery program:

- **Opinion 1 - Judgmental opinion:** This opinion states the adequacy or the inadequacy of the disaster recovery program based on the opinion of the review team after it has reviewed the program.

- **Opinion 2 - Attributes missing opinion:** This opinion does not cover the adequacy or inadequacy of the plan, but merely states what attributes of a good plan are present or missing. The opinion does not state whether the plan is inadequate because attributes are missing. The opinion leaves the final decision to the recipient of the report.

The most valuable of the two opinions is the first - a judgmental opinion. This forces the review team to make a positive statement as to whether or not the disaster recovery plan is adequate.

The judgmental opinion can appear in any of the following three formats:

- **Format 1 - Narrative opinion:** In this method, the review team describes the adequacy of the disaster recovery program in one or more paragraphs. The reviewer should speak in language understandable to his or her audience.

- **Format 2 - Qualitative statement:** In this judgmental method the review team uses a short expression to describe the adequacy. The most common expressions are:

  - More than adequate

  - Adequate

  - Less than adequate

  This qualitative opinion provides management a short assessment of the review team's opinion of the program. Note that this can be expanded by a narrative explanation of support for the qualitative opinion.

- **Format 3 - Quantitative assessment:** Under this method, the review team provides a quantitative score of the adequacy of the disaster program. For example, the perfect disaster program might receive a score of 100, and the numerical score given by the disaster recovery team is an assessment of its adequacy. Under this method, each part of a disaster recovery program must be weighted and then evaluated and given points based on its adequacy. The total points are accumulated to arrive at an adequacy score.

The recommended judgmental method is qualitative. Normally, it is sufficient for management to know if the disaster recovery plan is more than adequate, adequate or less than adequate. If the plan is less than adequate, management should be told why the reviewers believe it is less than adequate, and how it may be improved.

6.2   EVALUATING THE DISASTER RECOVERY PROGRAM

The evaluation of a disaster recovery program should be based upon the concerns identified in Figure 3-5. As stated in Section 3, once the review has determined whether or not the disaster recovery program adequately addresses these concerns, the review is complete. At that point, the assessment process is ready to begin.

The review program (Figure 3-5) stated whether the concern should be addressed using static, dynamic, or both types of testing. The static testing was primarily that of the internal control assessment (Section 4) and dynamic testing was done by evaluating the operational effectiveness of the disaster recovery steps through test processes (Section 5).

At this point, the results of both the static and dynamic tests should be documented and related back to the concern in question. **Figure 6-1, Evaluating the Disaster Recovery Program,** has been provided for this purpose. This worksheet can be used by the review team as a tool to help develop an opinion.

The recommended method for developing an opinion is a two-step process as follows:

Step 1 - Develop an Opinion About Each Individual Concern:

This requires the auditor to examine the results of both the static and/or dynamic tests to develop an opinion as to whether or not the individual concern has been adequately addressed.

Step 2 - Develop an Opinion About the Total Concerns:

All the individual opinions must then be consolidated to develop one final opinion about the entire disaster recovery program.

Figure 6-1 is designed for use in developing the individual opinions about specific concerns. The worksheet should be completed as follows:

No. (#):   The number of each concern that is being reviewed. This number comes from Figure 3-5.

Concern: Each of the concerns identified to be addressed during the review process should be documented on this worksheet. These concerns come from Figure 3-5.

Figure 6-1

EVALUATING THE DISASTER RECOVERY PROGRAM

#	Concern	Adequacy Of Control			Result Of Test	Opinion
		More	Adeq.	Less		

Adequacy of Control: The control assessment developed in Section 4 for each concern should be transcribed to this worksheet. The adequacy of control assessments were:

- More than adequate (More)

- Adequate (Adeq.)

- Less than adequate (Less)

This adequacy assessment can be obtained from the appropriate Figure 4-1 for that concern.

Results of Test: Based on the review plan, one or more tests may have been conducted to assess the adequacy of the plan to address each of the concerns. These tests and the method for assessing the results have been described in Section 5. As a result, an assessment has been made as to whether the results from the test were more than adequate, adequate, or less than adequate. The combined results of all the testing should be posted to Figure 6-1.

Opinion: The opinion of the review team should be based on the results of the static and/or dynamic test and the experience and judgment of the review team. However, the qualitative results of both the static and dynamic test can be helpful in both developing an opinion and supporting that opinion. If both the static and dynamic tests are considered adequate or more than adequate, the opinion of the reviewer should be that the concern has been adequately addressed. On the other hand, if either of those assessments are less than adequate the opinion of the reviewer will probably be that the concern has not been adequately addressed by the disaster recovery program.

6.2.1 DEVELOPING AN OVERALL OPINION

Once all the individual opinions have been developed, the review team is ready to develop the final opinion. This should be done by identifying all of the individual concerns that have not been adequately addressed by the disaster recovery plan (normally these will be the individual opinions that have been evaluated "less than adequate" in either or both the static or dynamic tests).

A listing should be prepared of all of the concerns which have not been adequately addressed by the disaster recovery program. The review team for each of these concerns should perform the following three steps:

Step 1 - Quantify the Impact of the Concern: Based on the information gathered during the static and dynamic tests, estimate the potential dollar loss that should occur to the organization in the worst case scenario for that concern.

103

Step 2 - Determine Significance of Worst Case Losses: If the maximum losses are significant, then the disaster recovery program should be considered inadequate. On the other hand, if the worst case is insignificant, then even though some of the concerns are not adequately addressed the disaster recovery plan should be considered adequate. If an inadequate assessment is determined, then it may be advisable to restudy the worst case scenarios to determine if they are realistic. If not, the assessment may be revised.

This exercise is helpful in explaining the final assessment. Putting these worst case scenarios into dollar amounts substantiates the opinion to management.

6.3   WRITING THE DISASTER RECOVERY REPORT

The final step in a disaster recovery review is to write a report describing the results of the review. While these reports should be written in a format and style customarily used in the organization, the report should include the following information:

Management Summary:

A one-page or less summary of the entire report highlighting the opinion, recommendations, and impact of the opinion and recommendations on the organization.

Scope of Review:

The report should identify specifically what the review covered. Without a fully descriptive scope, the reader of the report may be misled to assume some aspects of disaster recovery have been adequately handled (e.g., manual aspects of computerized systems) which in fact were not reviewed. It has been recommended that the scope be a summation of the identified concerns on Figure 3-5.

Background:

It is normally helpful to the reader to have an understanding of disaster recovery requirements and state-of-the-art in other organizations. This helps the reader put the report in the proper perspective for both the business and the industry.

Findings:

This section describes what the review team found as a result of conducting the review. Note that findings are both positive and negative in nature.

Opinion:

This key section of the report indicates the review team's opinion as to whether the disaster recovery program is adequate or inadequate, and why. Note that it is recommended that the opinion begin with a qualitative assessment of more than adequate, adequate, or inadequate.

Impact of Opinion:

If the opinion is "less than adequate" then it is important to indicate the potential dollar impact of that opinion on the organization. As suggested, this can be the worst case scenario, or it may be a range of impact from best case to worst case, or an average of best case, worst case. Regardless, the method of determining the impact should be stated.

Recommendation:

If the opinion is "less than adequate" then the review team is obligated to provide management with a recommendation on how to improve disaster recovery so that it will be adequate. When recommendations are made, they should also include the dollar cost of implementing the recommendation as well as the impact on people of implementing it (e.g., time requirements) and any impact on systems (e.g., changes made, software to be acquired, etc.).

If the opinion is "more than adequate" the recommendations may include suggestions to eliminate part of the disaster recovery program. For example, if some aspects such as backup contracts, additional off-site storage, appear unnecessary, the review team may want to reduce the disaster recovery costs, assuming that it can be done and still have an adequate disaster recovery program.

6.4   DISTRIBUTION OF DISASTER RECOVERY REPORT

The primary recipient of the disaster recovery report should be the individual responsible for the disaster recovery program. It is that individual who has the authority, budget, and responsibility to make changes to the disaster recovery program. If changes are needed, that is the individual whom the report should motivate to make the change.

In some instances only that part of the disaster recovery program relating to the following individual would be transmitted:

- Chief executive officer
- Chief financial officer
- Data processing manager
- Database administrator
- Computer operations manager
- User management
- Corporate security
- Corporate insurance department
- Corporate legal counsel
- Auditors
- Plant managers
- Physical security group

DISASTER RECOVERY PROGRAM EVALUATOR

SECTION 7

RELATED REFERENCES

(Selected by Permission from "Quarterly Bibliography of
Computers and Data Processing," Applied Computer Research,
P.O. Box 9280, Phoenix, Arizona)

BOOKS AND REPORTS

Auditing Computing Systems. FTP. 1978-. Variable paging. 3 Vols. $495.00.

A loose-leaf reference service providing information necessary to establish the EDP audit function, to outline the necessary tools, techniques, and approaches for use in auditing, and to suggest methodologies for management to evaluate the EDP audit function. Covers audit of applications, system design efforts, and computer centers with heavy emphasis on control practices. Updated semi-annually.

EDP Disaster Recovery: Planning, Implementation, and Procedures. FTP. 1981-. 2 Vols. Variable paging. $275.00.

A loose-leaf reference service covering the planning, management, and installation of an EDP disaster recovery plan. Management and personnel participation in recovery planning are discussed, and a procedures manual is included. Updated periodically.

Security: Data, Facility, and Personnel. FTP. 1982-. Variable paging. 2 Vols. $375.00.

A loose-leaf reference service written for the internal auditor and/or management's use in measuring adequacy of security in an EDP organization. Planning and implementation of EDP security measures are outlined. A checklist format covers both management and technical considerations including backup arrangements, company security, insurance, vital records security, physical security, personnel considerations, software considerations, operations considerations, and data communications. Sections are also included on costs, security hardware, and a bibliography. Updated periodically.

Security Evaluator. FTP. 1980. Variable paging. $125.00.

A loose-leaf reference service designed to measure the adequacy and effectiveness of an organization's security status. A series of questionnaires are used to evaluate system internal controls, input and output controls, on-line systems controls, fire and physical protection, personnel policies, use of outside services, and insurance coverage. An analysis of security costs is also included. Updated periodically.

Cafferata, O.G. and Lerch, L.A. **Disaster Recovery: What To Do Before the Unimaginable Happens.** CAN DATA SYS 15:38-9. FEB 83.

Describes an approach for preparing against disasters to data processing capabilities.

Defending Your Computer Room Against Disaster. MOD OFF 28:100+. MAR 83.

Contends that a plan is needed to protect data processing facilities from disaster and that a backup procedure is needed to take over when a facility is out of commission.

Ferry, Jeffrey B. **Auditing the Operating System.** EDPACS 10:1-8, APR 83.

Defines terminology and explains the concepts of the operating system and its subsystems, dealing with backup and recovery, data set, and database protection, passwords, audit trails, and terminal security.

Fine, Leonard H. **The Total Computer Security Concept and Security Policy.** EDPACS 10:1-20. NOV 82.

Discusses a computer security policy that addresses the definition of threats and risks, long-range security planning, operational security, disaster recovery planning and testing, and computer security roles and organization.

Friedman, Stanley D. **Contingency and Disaster Planning in the EDP Area.** TODAY'S EXEC. 5:PWS-10, AUTUMN 82.

Focuses on five major issues relating to the development of a sound disaster recovery plan: misconceptions over the scope of a disaster recovery plan; types and levels of potential disasters; disaster recovery plan vs. backup processing plans; contents of disaster recovery plans; and user disaster recovery plans.

Highland, Esther Harris and Highland, Harold Joseph. **A Guide to NBS Computer Security Literature.** COMP & SEC 1:164-76. JUN 82.

Provides a bibliography of special reports and technical studies in the field of computer security that have been published by the U.S. National Bureau of Standards.

Kleim, Ralph. **Disaster Prevention.** J SYS MGMT 34:10-1. MAR 83.

Contends that devastating losses to a company's data processing operations can be lessened or avoided by disaster prevention controls.

Shaw, James K. and Katzke, Stuart W. **An Executive Guide to ADP Contingency Planning.** COMP & SEC 1:210-5. NOV 82.

Provides the background and basic essential information required to understand the developmental process for Automatic Data Processing contingency plans.

Weights, Philip J. **A Methodology for Evaluating Computer Contingency Planning.** EDPACS 10:1-7. OCT 82.

Emphasizes the importance of adequate computer contingency planning based on a disastrous fire which claimed many lives and destroyed a portion of the data processing department.

Wong, Ken. **Quantifying Computer Security Risks and Safeguards: An Actuarial Approach.** INFO AGE 4:207-14. OCT 82.

Defines risk areas and potential losses in relation to computer security and contingency planning. The benefits of carrying out a business impact review are emphasized, and methods of assessing and controlling risks are described.